D0855991

Telling Lies
and
Getting Paid

Other books by Michael Konik

*The Man With the $100,000 Breasts
and Other Gambling Stories*

*Nice Shot, Mr. Nicklaus
Stories About the Game of Golf*

Telling Lies
and
Getting Paid
More
Gambling Stories

Michael Konik

Huntington Press

Las Vegas, Nevada

Telling Lies and Getting Paid

Published by
   Huntington Press
   3687 South Procyon Ave.
   Las Vegas, Nevada 89103
   (702) 252-0655 Phone
   (702) 252-0675 Fax
   e-mail: books@huntingtonpress.com

ISBN 0-929712-73-0

Cover Photo: Jenna Bodner & Bryan Haraway
Interior Design: Laurie Shaw
Production: Laurie Shaw

Printing History
1st Edition—March 2001

DEDICATION

*To T, who taught me more
than I was supposed to know.*

ACKNOWLEDGMENTS

Sometimes I stumble upon a compelling gambling story accidentally; I get lucky, like a guy trying to make a flush who catches two perfect cards for a backdoor straight. But more often I discover a tale worth telling thanks to a suggestion or hint from friends or colleagues. People like Duncan Christy, Jim and Susan Albrecht, and Steve Forte have steered me toward potential subjects, and I'm thankful for their wisdom and their taste.

I'm also thankful for the consistently good publishing work done by the crew at Huntington Press: Anthony Curtis, Bethany Coffey Rihel, Len Cipkins, and Laurie Shaw, who let my words live in print long after I've typed them. I reserve my greatest thanks and admiration for Deke Castleman, a sublime editor who knows when to raise and when to fold, when to dive headlong into the fray and when to merely watch. (I should be so smart.)

To all of you—and to all those interested in risk and reward, professional and amateur alike—I appreciate your contributions.

Michael Konik
February 20, 2001
Los Angeles

Contents

CREDITS

"Sister Jean Picks the Winners" originally appeared in Delta *SKY*. "The World's Greatest Backgammon Hustler," "Big Gin," "The Line Mover," "The Poker Flower," and "Holy Macau!," in *Cigar Aficionado*. "Home Poker" in *Poker Digest*. "High Roller" in *Where*. "Gambling Around the World" in the *Robb Report*.

The World's Greatest Backgammon Hustler

He doesn't have a permanent address. But Simon Jones isn't hard to find.

The Presidential Suites of the world's better hotels. The finest restaurants in Paris, London, and New York. The first-class cabins of trans-Atlantic airplanes. These are his usual domains.

Whether in a dark Moscow nightclub or on a technicolor Balinese beach or upon the pulsing streets of Rio de Janeiro during Carnaval, you can pick Simon out of the crowd. He's the one with the beautiful woman holding one hand and a little black briefcase in the other. The woman is, he'll admit, a frivolous accessory, one of the delightful spoils of being rich and generous. The briefcase, though, is another thing altogether. That briefcase is his life.

It contains a couple dozen polished ivory disks—"checkers," Simon calls them—two leather cups, four dice, and a cube with various exponents of the number 2 on each side.

Simon is the world's finest backgammon hustler. And

aside from the knowledge he stores in his head, his brief-case contains everything he needs to subsidize a life that seems shorn from the pages of an Ian Fleming adventure.

Simon Jones [his name and some identifying details have been changed] is in many ways a cipher, a phantom who occupies an all-cash shadow world that shields him from the scrutiny of inquisitive tax collectors and customs officials. But he is by no means obscure. Among the jet set, the preposterously wealthy businessmen and royalty for whom no luxury goes wanting, he is a regular fixture, as common a sight as a Bentley parked in the circular driveway of a European mansion. Simon is One of Them. And this, it seems, is the secret of his gambling success.

In *To Catch a Thief*, dashing and debonair Cary Grant plays a dashing and debonair burglar, a charming con man who mixes easily with his unwitting victims. Some years ago, I interviewed a man named Albie Baker, the international jewel thief whose story inspired the Cary Grant movie. The thief insisted his lock-picking and safe-cracking skills were only average—"There were hundreds of guys who could do what I did," he told me—but his people skills were unsurpassed. Dukes and Duchesses welcomed him into their social circles; politicians and city planners revealed their most secret confidences. All the while, the thief was relieving them of their precious metals. "Nobody suspected me, of course," the thief explained. "You don't suspect a member of your country club of burglary."

Simon's strategy is nearly identical. He has slept in the royal palaces of several Middle Eastern nations; he counts among his acquaintances the young (and reckless) scions of one of the world's largest distilleries and a major Italian bank; Hall of Fame athletes and Academy Award winners know his face. And all of them have sat across the backgammon board from Simon and happily watched him relieve them of their excess cash.

"All of these people, they like to be entertained," Simon remarks in the hushed clipped tones of a well-bred British school-boy. "I'm an absolute treasure to them. And, I suppose, they to me."

Simon is handsome in a non-threatening kind of way; he doesn't smolder, he comforts. His manners are impeccable. And though he's careful not to make a spectacle of himself, he is often considered the "life of the party," a well-bred Dionysus who happens to be quite splendid at an ancient board game.

The son of a career diplomat, Simon was born in Maryland, near Washington, D.C., but spent most of his youth in European boarding schools, reading James Bond novels instead of studying Latin. ("We should all be Bond," he is fond of saying.) After a nomadic year trekking through Nepal in search of something ("I can no longer recall exactly what"), Simon attended Cambridge, where he studied economics and psychology—disciplines that have prepared him well for his "career," if you can use such a common word to describe the life Simon has made for himself. He never took a degree. But it was at Cambridge that Simon discovered his talent for backgammon, a game that's ridiculously easy to learn, but ridiculously difficult to know.

"I played for fun, with a roommate, and I paid his rent every month with my losses," Simon remembers. "Somehow I found out that there were books written about the game. This struck me as something of a revelation, the fact that there might actually be a way to master the game beyond rolling a lot of good numbers. Without my friend knowing, I went to the library and read all the books on backgammon. Shortly thereafter, I was making more money in a day than most people make in a week of honest work."

In only a few months, after several profitable forays into private London clubs, Simon believed he could earn a living playing backgammon. "I knew I was the best player in Cambridge, and probably in the top ten or so in London. And since I had always harbored these juvenile Bond fantasies, I thought it appropriate to do something utterly irresponsible and impulsive and attempt to live by my wits."

Were this a movie, a banal morality tale promoting the virtues of steady employment and steadfast abstinence, Simon would have found himself beaten down by the cruel torments of reality, only to persevere the indignities of gambling-borne poverty and emerge several years later as a champion.

That's not what happened. Simon was a success.

He didn't become rich overnight, and his skills were not immediately commensurate with his tastes for fine wine and finer women. But at every level of competition he flourished. Simon began playing for the equivalent of $10 a point. Then $25, then $50, then $100. His rise came gradually—and, in his estimation, undramatically—his growing skills producing a growing bankroll. Now he's comfortable playing for $2,000 a point, some of the highest stakes in the world. Any higher and he feels himself starting to play conservatively, in violation of one of his essential rules: If you don't re-double [challenge your opponent to double the stakes] when you've got a demonstrable edge, you're playing too high. Given the chance to triple his net worth or go broke—for example, in a match against the Sultan of Brunei—Simon would take the chance.

He does not, however, view his occupation with wonderment. The romantic ideal that most amateurs harbor of the successful professional gambler is, accord-

4

ing to the world's greatest backgammon hustler, mistaken. "What I do is like selling insurance," he says. "You go to work every day. Some days are winners, some are losers. I try not to get too emotional about either result."

He has always been similarly sanguine about his talent. He recognized it early, developed it fully, and uses it to earn a living. But he does not stand in awe of it.

"Backgammon is an open-information game," he explains. "There aren't any hidden cards. You can see when people, yourself included, make mistakes. If you're properly objective, you can assess your opponents' weaknesses. And more important, you can assess your own weaknesses."

In the late 1970s, only a few years after reading his first book about backgammon, Simon could identify the best player in London: himself.

His rise continued unabated, culminating with victories at the World Cup tournament and the annual World Championship tournament in Monte Carlo, the only player ever to win both. (He still attends most of the major tournaments, primarily to develop new clients.) Today, Simon is widely regarded by cognoscente as one of the top three backgammon players in the world. But, he insists, it's not pure playing talent that has made him the most successful backgammon player on Earth. His math skills, he claims, are average, probably equal to an accomplished ninth-grader. His ability to analyze a table situation (a "proposition," in backgammon parlance) is less the function of technical prowess than keen intuition. And, he freely admits, he has neither super-human resolve nor *cojones* the size of grapefruits.

"I pick my spots well. I'm not a gunslinger. I don't need to beat 'the best.' I'd rather play the guy who can't see, hear, or think. I want to beat the donkey," he says, chuckling.

"There are gentlemen—well, certain authors, for instance—that I consider geniuses, great theoreticians who don't care about money. If you offered them one billion dollars in exchange for ten points off their I.Q., they probably wouldn't do it."

He glances around his penthouse suite overlooking Central Park, and laughs. "Me? I'll take the money."

Simon has just finished playing a week-long match against a Pakistani fellow, a banker, whom he met at the Traveler's Club in Paris. The Pakistani fellow beat Simon out of $250,000. Simon is not unhappy.

"I'll eventually take this guy for a couple million," he says dispassionately.

He views himself as a walking casino, capable of absorbing losses, sometimes large losses, but playing all the time with an advantage. Even the most famous casinos on the Las Vegas Strip have a bad day, a bad week, maybe even a bad fiscal quarter. But in the long run, they tend to get the money. So does Simon.

And like the casino that trumpets the number of jackpot winners who have periodically emptied out the casino's slot machines, Simon doesn't hide his losses. He advertises them. "If one of my clients beats me, I want them to enjoy themselves and spread the word. I want people to know how beatable I am. I want people to think I'm not as good as everyone says I am. If they didn't think they had some chance of winning, why would anyone play me?"

In this regard, Simon is not a hustler in the traditional sense, like a pool shark who acts as if he's never seen a cue ball. His deception is far subtler. He tells potential opponents, "I'm too good for you"—and they, being highly successful titans of the globe, winners in the arenas of business and finance and power, are eager to prove him wrong.

Unlike poker, where higher stakes usually mean more talented players, high-stakes in backgammon don't necessarily produce better players. In fact, most professionals will tell you the big games are lousy with bad players. And for some reason, they say, Simon attracts them like a flower does a bee.

"The ten best pigeons in the world are desperate to play with him," one top professional complains. "Nobody else can get near them, and they're falling all over themselves to play Simon. In my opinion," the pro says, "he's not the greatest player. He's very good, I think, but not great. But he makes more money than anyone in this business, because he finds the games. Actually, that's not true, " the pro says, reconsidering. "The games seem to find him."

This assessment does not bruise Simon's feelings. "I played a guy last year. He lost a hundred thousand to me in four days—and he was truly happy. He thanked me!"

Sometimes good players become surly when lesser players beat them. It happens all the time at the poker tables and almost as frequently over the backgammon boards. This, of course, only alienates the "pigeons." Still, many allegedly "professional" gamblers, a number of whom are seriously deficient in self-esteem and are more concerned with inflating their egos than their bankroll, seldom miss an opportunity to snivel or whine.

Not Simon. "If a guy is going to swim up a waterfall to beat me, I congratulate him, and I do it sincerely. I tip my hat to him. Gambling is like hunting. If you're constantly chucking spears at people, you can't whine if sometimes you get one in your back."

Not long ago, Simon was particularly flush. He'd spent the previous month in Monaco, playing a Kuwaiti sheik who knew he couldn't win. On the other hand, he didn't mind losing $5,000 an hour to his newly discovered friend, as long as the laughs flowed as freely as the first-growth claret. This particular sheik typically spends about $20,000 a day on hookers alone; the money he lost to Simon was, likewise, cheap entertainment.

With nearly $400,000 of the sheik's petro-dollars to the good, Simon traveled to Sweden for a tournament. There, one of the tournament directors challenged him to a match for cash. Knowing the guy had exactly zero chance of winning—"He couldn't possibly get lucky enough"—Simon readily accepted, *not* knowing that his opponent's playing stake was the money collected by the tournament to pay for the hall and awards dinner. Which is why Simon was mortified when the tournament official, down nearly $10,000 and belatedly realizing he had no hope of recovering, dashed for a nearby window ledge and threatened to jump.

"Of course, I immediately offered the man his money back," Simon recalls. "Well, now he *really* wanted to jump—honor and such. It was a rather tense moment, this man being several stories above Stockholm. So, instead, I offered to let him borrow the money. I assured him that he still owed me, that I wasn't letting him out of his debt. That I expected every dime. But that we could consider it a loan."

The tournament executive begrudgingly agreed—and has been paying Simon in small installments (an amount considerably less than Simon's monthly hotel tab) ever since.

"Looking back on my choice of profession, I could have made more money as a stock trader," Simon figures. "Much more than what I earn playing backgammon. But," he says, sighing contentedly, "I've met a lot of interesting people this way."

Sister Jean
Picks The Winners
2

Most Las Vegas gamblers would give their diamond pinkie rings to have the kind of handicapping success a Chicago lady named Jean Kenny has enjoyed over the past several years.

— Super Bowl XXVIII: She predicted Dallas would win by 17. They won by 17.

— Super Bowl XXIX: She predicted San Francisco would win by 20. They won by 23.

— Super Bowl XXX: She predicted Dallas would win by 14. They won by 10.

—Super Bowl XXXIV: She predicted Tennessee would shock Jacksonville and meet St. Louis in the title game, where the Rams would triumph by seven. Which they did.

—Super Bowl XXXV: She predicted (on "The Tonight Show With Jay Leno") Baltimore would thump the New York Giants. Cha-ching!

In 1994, as a panelist on WGN radio's "The Prediction Show," she compiled a 10-6 record, beating the host, Hub Arkush, and trouncing *USA Today's* odds expert, Danny Sheridan.

Jean Kenny, 46, credits her penchant for pigskin prognostication to good old-fashioned Christian virtues: hours of exhaustive research, concentrated mathematical analysis, and meticulous attention to details. She's got the kind of work ethic that is supposed to pave the stairway to heaven. During the season she reads *Pro Football Weekly*, a statistics-heavy periodical favored by wiseguy bettors, and the sports sections of the local *Chicago Tribune* and *Chicago Sun-Times*. She does her homework.

"I study the injury situation," Kenny says, showing me a six-inch-thick file of newspaper clippings. "I follow the key performers and track how they did in previous games. I keep a separate file on special teams [punt-return squads, for example]. And I especially like good defensive teams. I guess you could say I pay close attention to the NFL."

Actually, you might say Jean Kenny follows the NFL religiously. In addition to being a rabid Chicago Bears fan, an expert handicapper, and a trusted leader among the sports-betting crowd, Jean Kenny has been, for the past 29 years, a certified S.P.

As in, Sister of Providence.

As in, nun.

She teaches religion and drug education/prevention at Archbishop Weber High School in northwest Chicago, lives at the Immaculate Conception convent, and studies the Holy Scriptures for an hour every night.

Only when she's done with those solemn duties does Sister Jean Kenny study the stat sheets. She even writes poetry extolling the virtues of her beloved home team, Da Bears. Such as this little free verse paean: *And on the eighth day God said: "Let there be football!"/ And God created a classic team—the Chicago Bears.*

She is a most unusual individual, the kind of singular person most of us don't bump into very often: a lifelong nun who really, *really*, understands football.

The Sister Jean Kenny phenomenon is peculiar, but not entirely incredible, if you take into account the geographical influence: namely, that she is from Chicago. This is a town that takes its sports seriously—far too seriously. (I was born there; I'm allowed to say this.) Fans in Chicago are knowledgeable, passionate, and rabidly devoted to their beloved Bulls-Hawks-Sox-Cubs-Bears. These are fans who throw back opposing-team home runs at Wrigley Field. This is a city where every third billboard attempts to make a product tie-in with the Bulls' string of World Championships. This is a society of sports lovers who did not take "Saturday Night Live's" lampooning of Mike Ditka well, penning numerous letters of complaint to the NBC television network. This is where Michael Jordan lives.

Sister Jean Kenny is the unlikely end product of a Chicago culture that breeds sports fanatics—whether they're stockbrokers, truck drivers, or Sisters of Providence.

Her journey into the world of odds and pointspreads and over-unders began in 1985, when she won a William "The Refrigerator" Perry poetry contest sponsored by a local radio station. She had always followed sports as a child, playing varsity basketball and coaching tennis when she got older, but going to a Bears game, watching The Fridge rumble into the end zone—well, that gave her the kind of visceral thrill nuns usually derive from a particularly enlightening Bible passage. ("A good game is like watching poetry in motion," she says.) "Monday Night Football" thought their nationwide viewership might be amused by a Catholic nun's adoration of a 320-pound ball-carrying lineman and ran a segment about her during the 1986 playoffs. Shortly thereafter, Bears management invited Sister Jean to attend a few Bears games, where she got to meet Chicago's craven idol, Mike Ditka, he of the slicked-back hair, pugnacious jaw, and easily parodied motivational speaking style. Reporters started calling Sister Jean to ask her opinion of upcom-

11

ing football games; her predictions, it seemed, were often eerily accurate, as if touched by divine inspiration.

A spiritual leader, if you will, was born.

In addition to her regular Thursday-evening gig on "The Prediction Show," Sister Jean has appeared on KABC in Los Angeles, CNN, and "Late Night with Conan O'Brien." This year she premiered a new radio program, "NFL for Women," during morning drive-time. People pay attention to what she has to say.

"My motive is strictly fun," she insists, sitting in the living room of her Chicago convent home. "It's like a hobby, that's all. I don't personally bet on the games. Otherwise, something I do for fun would be like a Las Vegas carnival. You've got to draw the line."

The nice—and mildly surprising—thing about Sister Jean, is her merciful, even forgiving, attitude toward those who would sin. "If people want to bet on football games, fine," she says, shrugging. "I don't want to get into a big moral thing. If my listeners choose to bet, that's their business. If you take my advice and you're lucky, I'm happy. If not, I don't want to hear about it."

Sister Jean believes those who follow her advice will fulfill this quotation from John 16:22. "Your heart will rejoice with a joy no one can take from you." And if not, hey, she only does this for fun.

Sister Jean has received more than a few notes and calls from what she describes as "faithful" listeners who have profited from her advice. "Oh, I get calls all the time. 'I won twenty bucks because of you.' Or, 'Thank you for your advice. You really helped me win big.' Of course, I'm not so sure these people are going to be so happy if I make a big mistake. I try to tell people that betting on football games is a big risk."

She tells her fourteen-year-old students the same thing: She does a lot of study, she works hard on her handicapping, and she can strongly *recommend* certain picks. But ethics and responsibilities to a higher calling preclude her from plunking down the collection money on the Cowboys-Dolphins game.

"The fact that I'm pretty good at what I do gives me credibility," she says, nodding. "The kids really open up to me. They think I'm cool."

I can't help wondering, has Sister Jean ever considered establishing a "900"-line, like so many other "professional" touts? The profits could go to her diocese or some other worthy charity. She could advertise in the sports section of the *Trib*: "Sister Jean's Football Picks. There's Nun Better!"

"Oh, heavens no," she laughs. "I wouldn't do something like that even if I was allowed, which I'm not. I don't think it's right. And besides," she says, smiling, "if predicting football games ever became more than my hobby, it would stop being fun."

In lieu of monetary rewards, Sister Jean Kenny's handicapping prowess has earned her a scrapbook full of celebrity mementos, such as personal notes from Conan and his former sidekick Andy Richter, arm-in-arm photos with Bears star Chris Zorich, and her most prized picture: a shot of her with The Pope of Chicago Sports, The Man himself. Ditka.

"I'm very fond of him," Sister Jean says reverentially. "He's very feisty, but very likeable. And he knows his football. I think Mike Ditka is great. Of course, I generally like disciplinarians."

Meeting him was, she admits, the second biggest thrill of her life. "The first was Mother Teresa. That was the greatest moment of my life. But Ditka was a close second."

Big Gin

Contract bridge is too complicated. Poker can be too expensive. And pinochle involves a weird deck. By default, though there are no definitive numbers to prove it, gin rummy may be America's most widely played card game.

Whether gathered in basement rec-rooms or country-club dining rooms, millions of us—25 million to 40 million, according to some estimates—derive a disproportionate amount of pleasure from making melds, "knocking," and "going out." Like backgammon or checkers, gin rummy is a simple game to learn—my great-grandmother taught me how to play when I was six—but a difficult one to master. So although most amateurs know the basics (get rid of unmatched high cards, don't give your opponent two cards of the same rank or suit, etc.), few of us would be willing to stake our reputations, or much of our money, on our gin rummy expertise.

But some people would.

They are salesmen and plumbing contractors, car dealers and liquor-store owners. They are regular fellows from all walks of life and every part of America. And they play the game of gin rummy with a sophistication, flair, and insight that could send a stubborn opponent into Chapter 11.

Top gin rummy players, like John Hainline, a greeting-card distributor from San Francisco who has won more than 30 gin rummy tournaments and is widely considered one of the two or three best players on the planet, say that there's less luck in gin rummy than poker. "Sometimes a sucker can end up with all the money in a poker game," Hainline comments. "In gin, the good players tend to separate themselves from the field pretty quickly."

Hainline, who many years ago played on the PGA Tour, learned the game in the early '60s, after a practice round at Colonial Country Club in Forth Worth, Texas. "I lost about a hundred dollars to a couple of elderly gentlemen," Hainline recalls. "That was a lot of money to me back then, and I figured I better learn enough to get it back."

The floundering golf pro spent his night on Tour dealing out gin hands to himself, memorizing the percentages, and recognizing the recurring patterns in something like 66,000 different kinds of hands. That was the first step in making himself into a master.

Today, Hainline won't reveal his secrets, but he hints that he plays "differently" than his opponents, who, he says, can be easily categorized into "passive" and "aggressive" types. "I try to work all my hands in combinations," Hainline says, "low, medium, and high." He smiles slightly. "If I said any more, I'd be giving away too much."

Up until the late '80s, gin rummy tournaments around America flourished, attracting as many as 400 competitors. But as poker tournaments became more popular, gin rummy lost the influx of eager new players who, as in all gambling ventures, must replace those that consistently lose and, therefore, eventually fade away. Even non-gamblers have heard of the World Series of Poker. But almost no one outside of the gin rummy community knows that there are currently annual gin tournaments that award hundreds of thousands of dollars in prize money.

Several years ago at the Maxim Hotel and Casino in Las Vegas, about a hundred of the world's best players competed in the largest and most lucrative gin rummy tournament ever, the International Gin Rummy Tournament of Champions, which offered more than $250,000 in prize money. Enough lawyers, doctors, builders, bankers, investors, retirees, and professional gamblers entered the tournament to instantly make it the world's richest gin game. After four days of drawing, discarding, and laying down, Bill Ingram, 62, a real-estate broker from Rockwall, Texas, was awarded the biggest first place check in the history of the game: $100,000.

Similar, albeit smaller, gin rummy tournaments pop up around Las Vegas several times a year. These congregations tend to attract a core group of competitors, the same hundred or so sharpies who play the game a wee bit better than everyone else in the world. If this recurring group of sharpies is any indication, the typical gin rummy maven is male, middle- to retirement-aged, balding, bespectacled, pudgy to corpulent, and possessed of an impassive *tabula rasa* of a face, worthy of ... well, a world-class poker player. And like the poker champ, these mnemonically gifted expert gin players know the percentages for every combination of hands; they can recall exactly what cards have been discarded and plucked; they have an eerie ability to predict when their opponent is about to knock or when he is going for gin; and they even extrapolate information based on how an opponent arranges his cards. As one pro told me at a recent gin tournament, "When I'm playing gin rummy, it's like my opponent is drawing me a picture of his hand."

Not surprisingly, the man long considered the greatest gin rummy player in the world, Stu Ungar, also won the world championship of poker, the World Series of Poker, three times. Blessed with what many claim was an authentic photographic memory, Ungar's standard gin rummy proposition was this: Play him for any amount of money; when you were done you got back 10% of your losses. He had very few takers.

Due to a debilitating drug addiction, Ungar's legendary powers gradually faded, and he died several years ago in a squalid Vegas motel room. (Though registered for the Tournament of Champions and the 1998 World Series of Poker, he failed to show up for either event.) Now the title of Greatest Gin Rummy Player in the World, which once was seldom contested, could be fairly applied to a handful of consistent gin rummy winners, such as Hainline and Nevada's Norman La Pere. It's a mythical title, since there isn't really an organized world championship of gin rummy. But capturing the Tournament of Champions or, for that matter, any of the other smaller gin rummy tournaments, bolsters a player's claim to the honorific.

The man behind most of America's big-money gin tournaments is named Glenn Abney, though he's widely known simply as Mr. Gin. "I've been involved in the biggest, most prestigious, gin rummy events for the past four decades," he says, smiling contentedly. Abney, 72, has won more than 20 gin tournaments in his career, including the International, a 1,000-player extravaganza that flourished in the '60s. At one time, before Stu Ungar, he was recognized as the game's most fearsome and visible player. (His belt buckle and license plate say MR GIN;

his wife's, MRS GIN.) Abney learned gin rummy from his mother, who, he claims, left a poker game to give birth to him. "I was literally born with card sense," Abney says.

An enormous man with enormous appetites, some time ago Abney went on a controversial diet that relied on, among other things, an unapproved supplement. Big Glenn didn't lose weight. But he did lose a gin rummy player's most vital tool: a good memory. "My long-term memory is pretty much shot. But I can still remember the cards!"

Despite his travails, Abney can recall gin rummy games from "the good old days," back when a man like he could find a juicy game in any town at any time. "Most sociable gin games are played for a penny a point, a tenth of a penny a point. When I was a caddie at the Bel-Air Country Club, in the forties, maybe you'd hustle guys for ten dollars a game," Abney recalls. "Now there are gin games where twenty-thousand is at stake."

For Bill Ingram, at the International Tournament of Champions, even more than $100,000 was on the line. Throughout a tumultuous 24-year period, the voluble Texan had what he describes as "a terrible compulsive gambling problem, which cost me three wives, a business, and most of my friends." It was during this tortured phase of his life that Ingram learned to play gin rummy. "I wasn't much of a player to start. I just liked the action. But after I got my life under control, my game started to improve. For years I didn't gamble a nickel. Now I try to do it in moderation."

If Ingram's triumph at the Tournament of Champions were made into a movie, the critics might dismiss his story as too fantastically improbable. The tournament, like most organized gin rummy competitions, was set up so the cream could eventually rise to the top. The preliminary qualifying rounds saw the card sharps playing 16 games to 200 points (a gin or an under-knock were worth 25), with all 11-game winners advancing to the semifinals. After two days and approximately 10,000 hands of gin rummy, nine players representing nearly every region of the United States had qualified for the money round. Eleven others had 10 wins and had to undergo a one-game playoff.

Bill Ingram had won only seven of his first 13 games. Then, defying the odds, he won his last three matches to squeak into the playoff. Among the 10-game winners, one player, picked at random, got a bye directly into the next round. That was Bill Ingram.

In the quarter-finals he plowed through two tough matches, earning a spot in the final four. There, he narrowly defeated the prohibitive favorite, John Hainline. "I got real lucky against John," Ingram conceded. "Mathematically, he should have beat me. He's the best."

Hainline, incidentally, agrees. "When we sat down to play, he said what most opponents say, 'Oh, no!' That should be my nickname: 'Oh No!' Most guys tend to play too defensively against me; they get intimidated. But," Hainline says, shrugging, "you can't win 'em all."

Ingram's unlikely victory propelled him to the $100,000 championship match, a one-game 500-point marathon against Jeff Mervis, a professional card player from Sherman Oaks, California. Mervis was named Best-All-Around Player at the 1993 L.A. Poker Classic and regularly places in the money at major gambling events around the country. But he hadn't played in a gin rummy tournament for a decade.

The drama that had characterized Ingram's previous victories was conspicuously absent. To begin the contest, Bill Ingram was dealt a series of what seasoned players call "no-brainers," decision-less beauties that quickly lead to gin. He won the first nine hands, vaulting to a 351-point lead before Mervis could score a single point. In gin rummy parlance, Ingram had his man "barbecued."

"My strategy was to play wide-open offense for the fist four or five cards, giving myself a chance to make gin," according to Ingram. "Then I moved to the defensive, mousing down [reducing the hand's point total] and knocking. It may have looked like I was getting real lucky, but I like to think luck is just the product of preparation." Whether because or in spite of his methods, Ingram dispatched Mervis 500-127.

Prior to the tournament, only the 10th he had played in 11 years, Ingram had told his wife he was "going into training" and that he fully expected to win the championship. "I work a hundred hours a week on my business, and I play once or twice a month at the Walnut Creek Country Club in Dallas. The world-class guys at the tournament play every day. The first time I faced competition this tough I made a gazillion mistakes. So I got out all my old books, like Jacobi's *How to Win at Gin Rummy*, and I memorized entire passages. Let's just say I came here very focused. Very ready to win."

And thanks to the kind of gin rummy skill we amateurs can barely comprehend, he departed Las Vegas $100,000 wealthier.

Bill Ingram subsequently disappeared from the gin rummy scene. "Everyone seems to be vanishing," Abney remarks wistfully. "You may notice that there aren't many youngsters playing in this tournament," he says, surveying the Maxim's flourescently lighted ballroom.

"Most of the really great players are dead—and if they're not, they need to write down the cards."

Still, you don't have to look too hard to find a gin game. Most country clubs in America—particularly those in the two Palms, Springs and Beach—have a game going every day of the week. You'll find gentlemen like Abney and Hainline there most afternoons. They'll be sitting beside other aging men, whose graying hair and expanding waistlines conceal a computer-like mind working through the probabilities. Some of these fellows may be the undisputed champion of their golf club, or Moose lodge, or senior-citizen's center. And if they fancy themselves good and brave enough, they might wind up one day in Las Vegas, playing gin rummy for $100,000.

Home Poker 4

The fancy, slightly spurious, term for guys doing fun things together is "male bonding," a label that simultaneously embellishes and trivializes what guys do in groups. Sure, when a bunch of men sit around and watch a football game, scratching and burping and hollering, it is vaguely reminiscent of a tribe of hunters watching the antelope migrate across the African grasslands. And yes, when a bunch of grown men run around and have a game of pick-up basketball together, the sight recalls a bunch of not-yet-overweight-and-balding boys frolicking in their youth, celebrating their childhood.

But all this male-bonding stuff is essentially about play, about playing. Men like to play.

You've surely read a magazine article or two (or two hundred) explaining how our modern techno-driven world has robbed us of our playtime; how men have been figuratively castrated by everything from feminism to the computer; how difficult it is for boys to be boys (except, perhaps, in the armed forces). Blame it on whatever, the writers postulate, men have forgotten how to play.

For some browbeaten fellows, it might be true. But many others, such as the group of trend-ignoring guys I get together with, do indeed play. Regularly, and with great vigor. My guys convene on a playground filled with everything that excites a man: the thrill of the hunt, competition, good sportsmanship, power, grace, imagination, courage, and equanimity. For a few hours every week, my friends and I feel ineffably boyish and swaggeringly mannish.

Our playing field is not a jungle of the weedy or asphalt type. In fact, nothing about our playtime with the guys involves getting back to nature or beating totemic drums. Our time among men is spent around a table.

A poker table.

The poker table is one of the few places remaining in our impermissive society where guys can unabashedly be guys, doing the quintessential guy thing among a bunch of other guys. For it is at the poker table that a man best expresses what kind of person he is. The same has been said about the golf course, but anyone who plays both games knows how much more seriously men take their poker. So elemental is the game's hold upon us that most men would rather admit to being a lousy lover than an inadequate poker player.

At the risk of waxing lyrical about poker's spiritual qualities—many have suggested it is a microcosmic model of life, which may or may not be going too far, depending on the scope of your life—I will say this: Attending a regular home poker game is possibly the most fun a bunch of guys will ever have, save for activities that involve women in various states of undress.

Before an all-points-bulletin goes out to the Sexism Police, consider this: Even when your poker game includes women, they too, over time, become one of the guys. After a while they'll start telling off-color jokes and using distinctly un-ladylike synonyms for genitalia. Though an all-female game clearly has its charms, including a woman or two in your congregation of men will not damage the elemental guyness of your card night.

Be aware, though, that not only do women play poker often, seriously, and well, they frequently beat the pants off their male counterparts—literally, if they're playing the time-honored "strip" version. In the past several years, women have won events at several major poker tournaments, including the World Series of Poker, where the large fields are predominately male.

Most men, it seems, have difficulty playing against women. Too many otherwise accomplished card players let their testosterone cloud their judgment. They can't cope with the fact that a smaller, prettier, and often smarter person—a woman—could beat them in a game that is so much about power. They choke on their own machismo. All of Las Vegas' top female poker players have encountered the standard insults from insecure men and have learned to use their opponents' psychological weaknesses to their advantage.

Indeed, the best female poker players like to play with men; they thrive on the sexual tension. Some women, usually lesser players, prefer "ladies-only" games, where men are forbidden and the queen outranks the king. My 85-year-old grandmother played for years in a "girl group," where the stakes were tiny and the chatter abundant. Being a well-seasoned sharpie, my grandma usually won several dollars in nickels, which, she said, made her feel awful—taking money from other ladies being anti-social and all.

I would discourage inclusion of women in your home game. They will probably end up with too much of the winnings.

If you do include a woman in your group, remember: The cards have no regard for sex; they'll just as soon make a straight for a woman as a man—only it will sting worse if you have a scrotum.

How, then, should you construct your home poker game? Like a house in which you plan to live in for a long time—sturdily, with an eye toward the future. As with a savings account or a fling on the futon, you take out of a home poker game what you put in. Plan it well and you can look forward to many evenings of convivial camaraderie; slap it together haphazardly and a few weeks later you'll be stuck home alone in front of the television watching "Matlock" re-runs.

The best poker games are weekly affairs. Given our responsibilities as husbands, fathers, or cads-at-large, more often is logistically imprudent. If your game is good (and it will be, because like Tiger Woods on an off day, even when poker's bad it's good), you'll want to play more frequently. Like every night. But that's the path of the wicked, a sure way to ruin a marriage, not to mention your sense of anticipation. Treat the game like dining out at a fine restaurant: If you did it every night of the week it wouldn't be as sublime—and you probably couldn't afford it, anyway. The game should be your weekly treat, a recreational reward for being a swell and diligent guy the other six nights.

Conversely, if you play less often than once a week—say, once every two or three weeks—you'll find yourself crossing days off the calendar like a convict doing hard time. The poet and novelist, A. Alvarez, whose book *The Biggest Game in Town* is a classic chronicle of the Las Vegas poker scene, has been known to turn down dinner invitations from no less than Alfred Brendel because the proposed date fell on Tuesday, his beloved poker night. "At my age," Alvarez told an English radio audience, "there are very few thrills left." Mountain climbing, reading, writing, even sex—the frisson has dissipated. "But on my poker night," Alvarez said, "well, I know I'm going to enjoy myself, win or lose. My poker night is the only guaranteed enjoyment left in my life."

While such admissions are best not made to the wife, they are, for most men, disturbingly true.

Anthony Holden, the British journalist and author of the splendid memoir *Big Deal: A Year as a Professional Poker Player*, has participated in the same weekly game with Alvarez for more than 20 years. Holden reports members of his "school" (as he so Britishly puts it) have skipped social events at Buckingham Palace because they conflicted with the sacred Tuesday Night. "Nothing, but nothing," Holden says, "is allowed to get in the way of the game."

Like most home poker games, Holden's roster of participants includes a disparate mixture of men from all strata of the professional bedrock. Their only unifying bond—beside their fanatical love of the game—is that none of them have traditional day jobs. The game I played in regularly for several years boasted a similar collection of self-employed layabouts: an architect; a mortgage broker; a former bond trader; a photo stylist; an accountant; a restaurateur. With a line-up like this, a game can easily last until the wee hours of the morning, when only the lonely should be up and about, listening to Frank Sinatra records. Of course, no matter what time the game officially "ends," the losers will always clamor for "just another hour." (Don't snicker; you'll do it one day, too.)

Your game will probably include some upstanding members of society, so you'll want to end sometime before the bakeries start making their morning deliveries. So you should start early.

I've found that a home poker game needs about five hours to ripen fully. The most exciting action may happen early on (though often it doesn't), and the later hours sometimes degenerate into an ugly exercise in the winners protecting their stacks and the losers desperately trying to recoup. But on the whole, your poker game needs a shape. Each evening needs to find its theme, its dramatic arc. Also, some of the game's best conversation occurs after the players have overcome their initial excitement and, perhaps, anxieties.

As Tony Holden described in *Big Deal*, beyond demonstrating one's ingenuity with the cards and the eternal joys of deception and bluff and psychological warfare in general, much of the home game's fun lies in the elegant barbs that fuel the table talk. While your congregation of guys may never be confused with the Algonquin's, opportunities for aphorisms, epigrams, and knowing allusions abound. Playing with Holden once in a Las Vegas tournament—we are both frequent visitors to Binion's Horseshoe, home of the World Series of Poker—I was the recipient of a Shakespearean taunt perfected at Holden's Tuesday Night game. I had made a sizable bet. Holden looked me up and down like a cut of meat he was inspecting at the butcher's shop and proclaimed, "Thou wretched, rash, intruding fool ..." whereupon he picked up a huge pile of chips, as if to re-raise me, and said, "Farewell!" as he tossed his hand into the muck instead.

Too many *Hamlet* references, however, and you may find your game deteriorating into an effete culture klatch better suited to an afternoon tea party. What you will mostly talk about are the two most fascinating subjects in a man's life: sports and women, probably in that order. Politics, religion, and employment—basically anything that allows the mundane reality of regular life to intrude upon your weekly parallel universe—all that stuff is off-limits. A running commentary on your opponents' play is also unwelcome, as are plaintive whines decrying your rotten luck. Stick to baseball and breasts, whenever possible. Political correctness is not necessary; in fact, the home poker game may be the last sanctuary of the tasteless indecent joke. Since so much of poker involves sublimated desires often associated with sexual issues (pursuit, power, dominance), blue humor is not only acceptable, it's encouraged.

Given that the talk often crosses into the realm of NC-17 thrillers starring Sharon Stone, you won't want to play in a PG-setting. Find a room bereft of children, televisions, and spouses. Traditionally, a home poker game's locale rotates among the participants' domiciles. Eventually, the group decides that they like playing best at one particular place—perhaps it boasts especially good lighting or accommodating seat cushions—and the game settles there.

My recommendation, though, is to find a private room dedicated solely to cards. My regular game in New York City took place in an Upper Westside brownstone, whose owner had converted the basement into a miniature card club, complete with working kitchen and bar. The walls were decorated with several dozen framed aces of spades from vintage decks, and the "library" (a modest compendium stacked along a display case) featured the greatest hits of poker literature: stuff by Alvarez and Holden, Herbert Yardley's *Education of a Poker Player*, and a satisfying array of tutorials.

While any number of instructional books can teach you and your gang how to play hold 'em and any other variation of poker, I recommend a series of primers by the authors Mason Malmuth, David Sklansky, and Ray Zee. In addition to having strong backgrounds in statistics, mathematics, and game theory, this trio of theoreticians also plays poker for a living. Their books include *Winning Poker*, *Hold 'em for Advanced Players*, and *Hi-lo Split for Advanced Players*. Novice to expert can glean something useful from these texts.

The legendary Doyle Brunson's weirdly punctuated *Super/System*, a 500-plus-page tome, is considered one of the bibles of the poker canon, and it is required reading for any aspiring player. Some of the information is slightly dated, but the general concepts and specific strategies are well worth considering. Filled with folksy anecdotes, it's also entertaining.

Our room in New York felt like an underground refuge, where we could play and laugh and compete without fear of interruption or embarrassment or reproach. A place to have fun.

Of course, the best place to play in the world is in Las Vegas, in the poker room of a well-managed casino. Your mission will be to recreate that experience as accurately as possible. Note, however: The games you probably played as a youth, seven-card stud and five-card draw, are no longer the most popular forms of home poker. Seven stud these days is often played high-low, with the worst (lowest) hand splitting the pot with the best (highest) hand. Five-card draw is mostly played for low only, and is called ace-to-five (the best possible hand in this game) or lowball. Both games, though, pale in comparison to Texas hold 'em, a variation of seven stud that uses community cards. It is the game used to decide the World Champion of poker, and your group will probably find it the most simple and complex form of poker you've ever played. Las Vegas cardrooms deal hundreds of hold 'em games.

Unlike the Vegas games, though, your home affair will be self-dealt, unless you choose to incur the unnecessary (but wonderful) expense of a professional dealer, who works for minimum wage plus tips—around $1 a hand from the pot's winner. In every other aspect of your game, do not skimp.

You'll need: a felt-covered table designed for at least eight players; plastic (not paper) Kem playing cards, approximately $15 for two decks; clay (not plastic) chips, which vary in price according to design; and a plastic box card, approximately $1, which gets placed on the underside of the deck to prevent flashing of the bottom card and unscrupulous dealing.

Green eye shades—in the bookkeeper visor-style—are strictly prohibited.

Your game should also be well-catered. An informal poll—I asked a handful of poker buddies their opinion—reveals that delivered Chinese has replaced cold cuts and corn chips as the most popular home poker food.

"You can eat right out of the box without making a mess," one mu-shu aficionado explained. "Sandwiches take two hands, and you're always dribbling mustard on the table."

Keeping the felt clean is the first rule of poker dining. Eating stuff you normally wouldn't eat at home is the second. Roast beef, cheese doodles, and Hershey Kisses are poker game staples; all, in a break from tradition, should be provided by the game's participants, not the host. This method discourages a weekly contest of "how low—and inexpensive—can you go?"

Soda and fake beer are the home game's preferred beverages, though the trend in Las Vegas poker rooms seems to be heading toward bottled water. Hard liquor, despite its image as a manly elixir, should probably be avoided or taken in small doses. Forget the romantic image of the hardened gambler knocking back a shot of Jack. Nobody boozes it up at the poker table these days, except the losers. Of course, indulging in a wee dram of a noble single-malt Scotch is profoundly civilized, if not necessarily prudent.

Phil Hellmuth, Jr., one of the great tournament poker players on the planet and one of the youngest winners ever of the World Series of Poker, drinks milk.

Cigars, like whiskey, are no longer de riguer; in fact, those who enjoy a good Cubano are usually asked to take the stogie outside. Chewing on both (unlit) ends, though, remains popular. There's something reassuring about murmuring, "I raise!" through a mouthful of tobacco leaf—or shrimp lo mein.

Where living arrangements do not allow for an optimal environment, local Rotary and Kiwanis clubs often rent out rooms that will suit your purpose. Or you can improvise. My brother once played in a game in Milwaukee that met around the boardroom table of one of the city's most prominent law firms. The high-backed leather chairs, he reported, were a treat, but the gang eventually found a different venue. Nobody wanted to play where the game had to end before 7 a.m.

Clearly a vague "few hours" won't be adequate for your game's fraternal atmosphere to develop. "Whenever" is also not a good time to plan to quit. Let the game go too long and your finely turned ripostes will deteriorate into low-grade abuse, like Don Rickles without the timing. As a rule, 7 p.m. until midnight or 1 a.m. is usually sufficient for the game's myriad conflicts to work themselves out.

It's also a sufficient amount of time for the inevitable unequal distributions of "luckiness" to achieve a certain balance. If one guy seems to be getting all the full houses in the first hour of play (or even the first three hours of play), rest assured his so-called luck will eventually turn as the evening ages. Over the long-term—we're talking thousands and thousands of hands—everyone will receive the same distribution of "good" cards and "bad" cards. The longer your session goes, the more this selection of winners and losers will equalize.

Perhaps the most compelling reason for playing late—until midnight, at least—is tradition. Legions of men have slunk into their bedrooms well past curfew, prepared to feel the wife's wrath; hordes have stumbled into work in the morning after a lengthy poker game, bleary-eyed and maybe a little giddy. Every man should have the experience at least once, if not once a week.

Just as the regularity of your game's schedule will bring comfort to what will soon feel like "the rest of" your life, so too will the regularity of playing with the same familiar faces. Over time, your game will develop its stars, guys whose superior play or force of personality lend your congregation a distinct flavor; other players will settle comfortably into supporting roles, content merely to be part of proceedings. The game's success, like a dinner party or an episode of "Cheers," hinges on the chemistry of its participants. It is truly an ensemble effort.

The optimum number of players for your weekly fete is eight. Every standard poker game—i.e., those that do not involve sticking cards to your forehead or making every odd-numbered denomination wild—can be played comfortably eight-handed. Many green-baize-covered tables are specifically designed for eight players, and even those that aren't can be made to accommodate this number.

If you cannot achieve this quorum, five is the absolute minimum to generate a worthwhile evening of cards, conversation, and camaraderie. When the game gets short-handed, the danger of one player absorbing the brunt of the losses becomes magnified, which will shrink your numbers by at least one more.

Of course, the game's composition—the guys who are its regular participants—is the most important factor in determining how long and prosperous it'll be. Give your game at least ten sessions to mature before you start tinkering, but don't start calling it "regular" until it's been up and running for at least a year. Decade-long streaks are not uncommon; some home games flourish until too many of the competitors become ill, senile, or die.

When assembling your group, pay close attention to two seemingly opposing goals: Simultaneously aim for eclecticism and egalitarianism. A various, almost odd, collection of players will imbue your game with the kind of endearing quirkiness that draws us to eccentric comedians. There's something wackily enjoyable about spending one evening of your week with people from walks of life you normally don't tread. Where else but the poker game can an abstract-expressionist sculptor (who works in soft metals and favors the writings of Engels and Robbe-Grillet) mingle comfortably with a senior partner of a white-shoe law firm? No one wants to spend his playtime with the same half-dozen guys he works with, anyway. Treat your game as easy-to-digest sociology, a chance to see how the other seven-eighths live.

On the other hand, you'll want your ensemble to be a collection of equals—equals in skill, in financial well-being (or lack thereof), in fortitude. "It is a statistical and fiscal truth—it has to be—that the same seven or eight people cannot play poker together every week for twenty years unless the money runs back and forth in fairly equal proportions," Tony Holden writes in *Big Deal*. As the years pass, a handful of peripheral players will come and go, but the core group, if assembled properly, will remain. This nucleus provides the game's cohesiveness and its spark. And if it is not comprised of players with reasonably equivalent power—especially spending power— the game will disintegrate.

Which bring us to that prickly question: How much should you play for?

The answer is equally prickly: Enough to hurt.

Poker, unlike any other game, uses money to keep score. If your stakes are set too low, the game degenerates into a lottery, where eight adults sit around all night, calling all bets and seeing who gets dealt the high hand. That's not poker; it's Go Fish. If the elements of bluff and leverage are removed, you rob the game of the skill and judgment elements, which, over time, separate the winners from the losers. You must play for high enough stakes that a potential caller will have to pause to consider the consequences of his action if he's wrong. And those consequences have to be harsh enough that wild throw-your-money-in-the pot-and-see-what-happens poker is soundly discouraged.

Vegas professionals make a living off such games; you're not a Vegas professional. Vegas professionals do not view the poker room as a merry place to hang out with the boys; they see it as the office. Whereas they dream of weak games, where unschooled chumps holding little more than fantastic dreams contribute to pot after pot, you want parity, something solid, a game that won't evaporate because the bad players have run out of money or gotten smart. Unlike the professional, the home maven plays to have fun. That's the point of the game: to play, to socialize, to frolic. But, quixotically, the game isn't fun if played for piddling stakes.

Thus, the stakes should be set so that if you lose, you'll care. Conversely, if you win, you'll want something to show for your efforts. Since every part of your game should encourage its promulgation, start modestly, lest you "ruin" potential playmates in only a few sessions.

You might have to experiment to find out how high, or low, your group wants to play. Be flexible at first: Start low and move up. As a general rule, to gauge what kind of win-loss swings you might expect at various levels of wagering, multiply the biggest bet in the game by 25. If, for instance, you're playing $2-$4 hold 'em, a profit or debit of $100 would not be unusual. In a $10-$20 game, be prepared for swings approaching $500. In no-limit or table-stakes games, your swings can be as big as your entire bankroll.

These are very broad measurements. The standard deviation for every game is different. Based on your skill, or lack thereof, and that of your opponents, your expectation may be considerably larger or smaller. If you consistently find yourself winning or losing more than the 25 multiple, either you or your game may be getting a mite out of control.

The best rule to determine your stakes is this: Do not play for more than you can comfortably afford to lose.

Or win. Consistently winning more in your home poker game than you earn at your day job can have a dire effect on your work ethic.

I played for a few years in a no-limit game, where whatever amount of chips you had on the table was your betting limit. Thousand dollar pots were not uncommon. But players willing to compete at that level were. The game suffered through month-long droughts of inactivity, when the festivities had to be postponed due to a lack of fresh warm bodies.

Play for an amount that quickens your breath a bit, but doesn't leave you breathless. The exact numbers are up to you and your pals and your respective bankrolls. But no matter your tax bracket, I suggest using the Wife Test to find the proper level: Play at least for an amount that if you were to lose, you would be hesitant to tell your partner.

For some men it's a few shekels; others need tens of thousands on the line before they feel a pulse. (That's why they have the World Series of Poker.) Despite the myth of America being a classless wonderland, the state of our egos is still inextricably tied to the size of our wads (the monetary one). For the sake of class-conscious pride most men find themselves playing in a game that's actually a bit too big for them. Employ the Wife Test and you can avoid this trap. Remember, the money (all in cash and putatively tax-free) is secondary to the fellowship.

Since funds will change hands at the end of the night, your group must establish beforehand how and when payment should be made. One important piece of advice: While allowing players to carry a tab is gentlemanly and exhibits good faith and all that, don't do it. When the evening ends, pay up. Adhere to this policy strictly, or at some point you'll feel like Citibank trying to collect from a developing South American republic. Cash is preferable, but if your game's limits are nearly as lofty as your city's crime rate, checks may be acceptable.

Assuming everyone in your game will be a friend, or at least a friend of a friend, the occasional bounced check, though inconsiderate, can be tolerated. When someone *defaults* on a payment, however, your game must be equipped to deal with the culprit.

The debtor should immediately be banished in perpetuity—even if he intends and eventually does make good on his transgression. Anyone who loses, writes a check for what he owes, then stops payment is a low-life scoundrel or is playing for much more than he can afford. In either case, he's not someone who belongs in your group. Though every game has its own rules for dealing with bad debts, I recommend this one: If a player screws the game, all regular participant help to absorb the loss.

Not only does this method encourage good sportsmanship, it discourages your group from wantonly admitting a newcomer without a thorough and thoughtful examination of his character and reputation. You need fresh players; without them your game will suffocate as stalwarts move away or drop out. But include them cautiously, and only on the recommendation of one of the regulars, who, for a brief probationary period, acts as the new man's sponsor.

Another reason you'll want to warn off neophytes is for *their* protection. Competing against a lineup of guys who have been playing together regularly and know each other's play intimately—Andy always checks when he's got a monster hand; Dave always starts talking fast when he's bluffing—even Doyle Brunson would have trouble winning. You're in the business of innocent amusements, not fleecing unwitting suckers.

An editor friend of mine likened the home poker game to a men's salon, simultaneously a place and an event, where men could congregate to talk, to play, to be themselves. I thought his metaphor was a good one, and proposed it one night to my group of gamblers. "Do you guys feel our game is the modern equivalent of a nineteenth century men's salon?" I asked.

The responses were an indecorous chorus of monosyllabic grunts, followed by the phrase most often heard at this kind of "salon": "Hey, come on already! Whose deal?"

So I posed the same question to Tony Holden, whose Tuesday night game features some of the brightest figures in British arts and letters, a constellation of learned and accomplished men, any one of whom you would probably be honored to spend an evening with. He replied, "A modern male salon? As we sit there squabbling—invariably over the pot being a pound or two short—my wife says we're like a bunch of old women. And she's right: But this is surely the ultimate tribute to middle-aged male bonders." Even over there, in the Land of the Bard, they would rather talk about poker than poetry. And they would rather play poker than talk about playing.

After a few sessions at the table with your crew of playmates, poker's charms will seduce you—the mental acrobatics, the imagination, the courage, the logic, the discipline, the thrill. You'll soon discover one of the great poker truths, a maxim that could just as easily be applied to the game of life as a game of cards. As the legendary gambler Nick "The Greek" Dandolos said after battling three-time world champion Johnny Moss in an epic, and ultimately ruinous, game of five-card stud: "The next best thing to playing and winning is playing and losing."

Getting Paid and Telling Lies: The Offshore Sports Book Industry

Nearly five years ago, back in the rosy days when I was an innocent lad uninitiated into the exquisitely dirty world of offshore sports gambling, I wrote about the then-nascent industry from the perspective of an outsider, a curious observer trying to make sense of a new wrinkle in the gambling tablecloth. Today I'm a wee bit wiser.

I didn't realize then that I was witnessing the inception of a milieu as unashamedly Machiavellian as any serious campaign for United States political office.

Back then I watched; now I play. Back then I was enthusiastic; now I'm skeptical. Back then I was blind; now, as the song goes, I can see.

And it ain't a pretty sight.

My original take on the world of offshore wagering, written in the mid-nineties, went like this:

It's as easy as buying a fruit basket.

You pick up the phone, dial a toll-free number[1] that

---

[1] Now, most offshore bookies can be reached instantly through the Internet as well.

connects you to an office in a faraway land, give the nice man on the other end your account information, and place your order. If you're lucky, a few days later your "merchandise" arrives in your mailbox. Only it's not strawberries and melons, but a certified bank check.

Welcome to the latest development in the world of sports gambling: offshore bookies.

While a sports-bettor's options were once confined to either the legal services offered in Nevada or the local but illegal bookmaker, gamblers can now bet quasi-legally by telephone with an internationally based operation. I say quasi-legally because it's a crime in most states for residents to make a bet on sports over the phone; on the other hand, the bookmakers operating out of locations as far flung as Australia and Antigua are fully sanctioned by their respective local governments.

According to Professor I. Nelson Rose from Whittier (California) Law School, a leading authority on gambling and the law, "The Interstate Wire Act makes it a crime for anyone in the business of gambling to use a telephone line that crosses a state or national boundary to transmit information assisting in the placing of bets. Note that the law applies only one way: It is not a federal crime for a player to make a bet by phone." In other words, it's the bookies who are breaking federal law. Some states, such as California, have passed even stricter laws, which prohibit accepting or making an illegal wager. Most experts agree, though, that law-enforcement officials are generally uninterested in busting bettors; they're focused on putting the bookies out of business.

As Rose notes, "True players—guys who aren't bookies—never get arrested for making a bet." A seasoned sports bettor who prefers to remain anonymous says, "Unless you're a monster bettor, the feds aren't going to bother you."

Establishing an account overseas is simple. After fill-
ing out an application verifying age and identity[2], gamblers deposit U.S. funds in the bookmaker's bank, either
via wire transfer or cashier's check; for a 3% surcharge
(often waived), most places even take credit cards. After
their account is activated, players are assigned a PIN
number. Many operations also offer hundreds of dollars
in incentives to new customers[3].

To bet, customers call the bookie's toll-free number,
identify themselves by code, announce their bet, and listen as the clerk calls the bet back. (All telephone calls are
recorded for mutual security.) A $50 minimum bet is re-
quired by most overseas operations. Maximums typically
range from $5,000 to $20,000 per bet, similar to Nevada
limits. If the player loses his bet, the money is deducted
from his account. If he wins, the proceeds may either be
reinvested in his account, like a dividend, or sent to
America via overnight courier.

At present (remember, I was writing in 1995), offshore
bookies accessible to American gamblers operate in the
Dominican Republic, Antigua and Barbuda, Aruba,
Grenada, St. Vincent, Venezuela, Curacao, Mauritius,
Australia, Belgium, Costa Rica, Panama, Belize, St. Kitts,
and Gibraltar. It's difficult to estimate how many opera-
tions exist—certainly hundreds—or how much money
they take in. One publicly traded company, Interactive
Gaming and Communications, which operates Sports
International Race and Sports Book in Antigua and

---

[2] A formality many operations no longer bother with.

[3] The industry standard is a 10% bonus on a player's initial deposit,
credited as cash directly into his account. Some companies occasionally advertise bonuses as high as 30%-40%, but these too-good-
to-be-true offers are often too good to be true. Several dozen notorious scammers, now out of business or operating under another
name, used the "we'll give you the moon" come-on before abscond-
ing with all of their customers' cash.

Grenada, reported gross wagers of nearly $50 million in both 1994 and 1995[4].

Michael "Roxy" Roxborough, the world's preeminent oddsmaker, whose company, Las Vegas Sports Consultants, supplies many of the offshore bookies with their betting lines, says, "It's hard to say how much money the offshore bookmakers are taking in altogether. Certainly more than all the sports books in Nevada, which handled $2.5 billion in 1995. It's got to be a huge number. Anyone can pick up the telephone[5]."

Terry Cox, formerly the race and sports book manager at Harrah's Reno, as well as at an offshore operation in the Caribbean, says, "The growth of sports gambling is phenomenal, whether legal or illegal. Offshore bookies are taking advantage of that growth by providing a more formal, structured, reliable scenario than the typical illegal bookie."

Cash-hungry foreign governments that collect licensing fees and taxes from the sports books not only allow the books, but encourage them. Indeed, in October 1995, Antigua and Barbuda's minister of communication sent an open letter of invitation to bookmaking companies, saying that his government was "keen to develop its offshore market sector, particularly the offshore gaming sector" and that Antigua was "the perfect spot to relocate your sports betting company[6]."

Years before Antigua rolled out the welcome mat, Ronald Sacco, a mob bookie known as "The Cigar," took his business to the Dominican Republic. Trying to out-

---

[4] They subsequently went out of business, leaving behind thousands of unpaid customers.

[5] Roxy has recently sold his interest in LVSC and no longer personally supplies opening numbers.

[6] Belize is the latest principality to court bookies, promising them government cooperation—not to mention cheap telecommunications prices.

run a series of felony convictions for bookmaking in the States, Sacco opened shop on the island of Hispaniola in the late 1980s, connecting to his old stable of clients via toll-free telephone lines. While the weather was hot, the pressure from law-enforcement officials was not. Sacco thought he'd found the perfect haven. But "The Cigar" was an old-time bookie who used old-fashioned methods for paying and collecting: a network of runners and clerks who made cash transfers back in America. (The new breed primarily relies on electronic or mail transactions, though some have so-called "agents" who recruit players and handle the collections and disbursements.) Sacco, apprehended on a return trip to the States, was convicted of money laundering in 1994.

But his cronies had seen the light—or at least a reflection of the light. A substantial number of operators with organized-crime ties (as well as prior convictions) transferred their businesses to the sunny Caribbean, where licensing fees cost as little as $5,000 (they now go for closer to $100,000) and background checks were nonexistent. They kept their wiseguy clientele and shadowy practices—no advertising, no publicity, no customer service— but took care not to make the same mistakes as Sacco.

While some offshore operations are still "mobbed up," in the past few years many international sports-betting shops have become more corporate. Run by former (legal) Nevada bookmakers and backed by venture capitalists and marketing wizards, these sports books advertise heavily in such mainstream outlets as airline in-flight magazines and issue quarterly earnings statements. Some are even publicly traded companies.

Which leads to an obvious question: Will the offshore bookies put the corner bookies out of business? Will they take a bite out of Nevada's legal sports-betting market?

"This is definitely the wave of the future," one major professional sports bettor tells me. "Everything is going

to depend on this new federal Gambling Commission"—
which was set up to examine the ramifications of gambling and make recommendations—"and Congress and
the Justice Department. If they all want to get involved,
things could get messy. But if everything remains status
quo—it's like it might as well be legal. Why would anyone want to deal with some goon with a paper bag full
of cash when he can do it so clean over the phone?"

The man who makes the odds doesn't necessarily agree.
"I don't think the illegal corner bookies will disappear,"
Roxy says. "The offshore bookies will hurt the illegal guys,
but not put them out of business, because the illegal bookies still offer credit and they probably have lower mini-
mums." Roxy thinks the offshore operations will have even
less impact on legal sports books. "The offshore operations definitely won't affect Nevada, unless someone suddenly puts a hundred thousand hotel rooms in Antigua.
Vegas sports betting is done mostly by tourists. The offshore bookie is going after a different customer."

Indeed, Roxy thinks that rather than eroding the exist-
ing market in sports gambling, the offshore bookies are expanding it. "We're seeing a whole new segment of sports
gamblers," Roxy says. "We're seeing professionals, successful people who like the security and discretion of the offshore bookies, people who might not be comfortable dealing with a mob bookie. For these players, the kind of gambler who reads the Wall Street Journal, doing business with
an offshore bookie is like calling their stockbroker."

Since no money changes hands on U.S. soil, you have
about as much chance of getting harassed for making an
overseas sports bet as you do for smoking a Cuban cigar.
This is why Scott Kaminsky, odds manager for Bowman
International out of Mauritius, says his business can only
get bigger[7].

---

[7] He's now the main man at LVSC.

"I don't know a single person who has ever been charged with as much as a misdemeanor for betting. The American government won't say it's illegal to bet with an organization such as ours, so you can almost assume they're implying it's legal[8]."

Kaminsky, whose office employs up to 100 clerks during the heart of football season, says offshore bookies are serving an enormous market. "We're helping make a billion-dollar industry become legal. It seems like two new offshore shops open every week. This isn't necessarily gambling's future, but it's definitely the present."

Offshore bookies offer American sports bettors several appealing improvements over the mob-connected bookies operating out of corner bars, such as:

- *Accessibility.* With toll-free 800 or 888 numbers manned by dozens of clerks, it's often easier to get a bet down with your man in the Caribbean than it is to reach a customer-service representative at your long-distance company. According to one major Las Vegas gambler, a man who can make phone bets legally in his home state, but prefers to deal with the international bookies, "I'd rather bet with some of these offshore operations. They run their business like a business. They treat you like they want your action. Try calling a Las Vegas sports book—they'll put you on hold for ten minutes. They act like they're doing you a favor. The offshore guys are all about service."

---

[8] As a gentleman named Jay Cohen can attest, the U.S. is becoming much more explicit in its displeasure with the burgeoning offshore gambling industry. Cohen, one of the founders of World Sports Exchange, a pioneering book in Antigua, was charged—and convicted—of violating the Wire Act. He is currently free on appeal. His case is viewed by many in the offshore gambling industry as both precedent-setting and foreshadowing with regard to either further legal travails or blissful freedom.

- *Different odds.* One of the keys to beating the bookies is getting a good "price," or odds, on your bet.
  Smart sports bettors shop around, looking for the
  best deal. If Vinny is offering the Packers as seven-
  point favorites and Sid has them at six and a half,
  players who want to take the Packers will opt for
  the bookie offering the half-point discount. Gamblers who play with offshore bookies can get a
  dozen or more different quotes on the game of their
  choice, ideally finding a bargain price. "The offshore
  books don't usually move their lines as quickly as
  the bookies in America," one professional sports
  gambler says. "I'm not saying you can find numbers that are outrageous, but sometimes you can
  find a good value."

- *Large menu of bets.* Ask your local bookie if he'll
  take your action on a European rugby match. Or a
  South American soccer game. Or a Japanese golf
  tournament. Chances are he'll offer action only on
  American football, baseball, and basketball, and the
  occasional fight. Offshore bookies, who cater to an
  international clientele, post numbers on just about
  anything, including elections. "The offshore bookies put up a lot of exotic bets, some strange propositions," the professional sports gambler says. "I
  don't know if they're good values—probably not—
  but if you're looking for unusual action, they'll give
  it to you."

Betting with offshore bookies can have its downside,
particularly if you wager large sums. "I believe that
ninety percent of these operations would be in trouble if
every one of their clients asked for their money at the
same time," says Roxy Roxborough. "A lot of these start-
up operations are living on the float. One bad football

month, four losing weeks in a row—and that can happen—you'll see a real shakeout."

There are other risks associated with offshore gambling. Among them are:

- *Getting stiffed.* While a telephone bettor has an assurance that his licensed offshore bookmaker won't be suddenly shut down by the government—as happens occasionally to illegal bookies—he is nevertheless faced with the very real possibility of getting ripped off. Most American bookies let their customers play on good-faith credit: You make your bet, then pay off or collect later. Offshore bookies, however, will let you bet only what you have on account. In other words, you've got to put up a lot of front money. Sending cash overseas to someone you've never seen—potentially a con man with bad intentions—clearly exposes you to fiduciary chicanery. "It's one thing to win a bet and not get paid," a serious sports bettor says. "To lose everything you put up, that's a catastrophe."

- *Odds.* Just as the variance in price quotes between your local bookie and a book offshore can work in your favor, it can also hurt you. "If you don't shop around, if you accept whatever odds an offshore bookmaker offers, you might be getting a bad price," Roxy Roxborough says. "On the other hand, if the odds are too good, you could be looking at a going-out-of-business sale."

- *Uncollectible debts.* Unless you're interested in flying to, say, Costa Rica to chase down a few hundred bucks, you'll have little recourse, legal or otherwise, to collect money owed to you. Whereas you can see your local bookie (or one of his runners), with an offshore office you're merely dealing with a distant voice on a telephone. Do your research well, because once you're screwed by an international bookmaker, you'll probably never collect.

When selecting an offshore bookie, look for these three attributes: quick and efficient payment, competitive odds, and courteous service.

"The whole key to playing with an offshore bookie is buyer beware," Roxy says. "Do your research. How long have they been in business? Have friends and colleagues reported good experiences? What's their reputation? Do they even have a reputation? Of course, this is the same common-sense approach you would use buying a used car or a vacuum cleaner."

Except buying a used car or a vacuum cleaner was never this easy.

That was then.

In the spirit of *caveat emptor*, let me tell you about now.

Of the hundreds of sports books operating offshore—and there seem to be a few new ones opening every week—I can recommend only a handful. The industry is plagued with problems.

Those who would like to see gambling banned on the Internet decry the lack of regulation and oversight enjoyed by the offshore gambling industry. Anti-Internet-gambling proponents say that millions of vulnerable victims must be protected from charlatans and con-men hiding behind glowing monitors, waiting to fleece any innocent Web surfer with a credit card. The pro-Internet-gambling forces say that's nonsense, that the cyber-gambling joints are legitimate businesses with the capital investment and ethics of any other dot-com. The fact is, in the case of the offshore sports book industry, the bookies are proving to be their own worst enemy.

By failing to police themselves effectively, they are inviting federal intervention. And I'm not sure it won't be warranted.

Presently, because many of the bookies are operating illegally in the eyes of the United States government and legally in the eyes of whatever principality the bookmaker calls home, disgruntled gamblers still have little if any legal recourse when they have a dispute with the guys holding the money. If an offshore bookmaker refuses to pay his customer, in most cases all the book stands to lose is its reputation. Now, that's a big deal in the world of bookmaking, where "honor" is considered as vital a commodity as a big bankroll. But to a disgruntled player, none of that reputation stuff can replace his missing cash.

As Bill Haywood illustrates in his book *Beat WebCasinos.com*, most offshore operators, whether Internet casinos or phone-in sports books, prefer to milk their cash-cow customers instead of slaughter them for meat. Therefore, outright larceny doesn't take place often. But when it does, the cow stays dead. The reality is, if an offshore bookie decides to steal a player's cash—for whatever reason—the player will have an awfully difficult time getting it back. Though there are relatively few outright thieves whose *raison d'etre* is to steal whatever money foolish gamblers send to them, there are plenty of what I term "reluctant stiffs," guys who originally had no ill intent when they opened for business, but turned rotten under pressure. These are bookies who, either because of mismanagement or personal failings, discover at some point that they don't have the funds to pay all of their customers. Unlike in Vegas or other highly regulated casino environments, there's no official body that monitors the amount of cash these sports books have on hand. Jurisdictions such as Australia and Antigua are supposed to have government agencies overseeing their books—and fewer bad shops exist in these places than, say, Costa Rica, which has no federal oversight—but even these countries don't guarantee a player's deposits. Sometimes when there's a "run on the bank," a wave of simultaneous withdrawal requests, the weaker operations simply don't have the funds to cover their obligations. Too often, regrettably, some of them take the easy way out.

And because few jurisdictions conduct criminal background checks or demand promissory bonds, deadbeat bookies can simply open a new shop under a different name, in a different locale, and try again.

It should be noted that, perhaps surprisingly, it's not always the little shops that are the most egregiously dishonorable. Often it's the Very Big Operations, the industry's VBOs, that are most dangerous. Some of the biggest and most heavily advertised books are in fact the worst places to play.

It's also important to note that the targets of many non-payment, or ridiculously slow payment, cases involve winning (often professional) bettors. Many of the biggest offshore bookies, as well as most of the smaller ones, dislike so-called "sharp" customers, players who will either win in the long run or lose less than the average degenerate sports gambler. Like casinos that banish card counters, many of the largest offshore sports books despise winning players. They'd much rather have their phone lines and bandwidth occupied by losers, just as most casinos would like their blackjack tables filled with people who will split a pair of fives and always take insurance.

I am one of these winning players, a professional gambler connected to some of the best information in the world of sports betting. As such, much of what I relate here comes from personal experience. In addition to several years of active research, betting on thousands of games with hundreds of offshore bookies, I monitor several online message forums, where players share information about good and bad operations. Since anyone can write virtually anything he wishes in an online chat room, I cannot vouch for the veracity of all the numerous complaints, cries of agony, and pleas for help that turn up regularly on Web sites dedicated to offshore sports betting. Some may be elaborate hoaxes or vicious lies. But not all of them. And based on my travails, as well as those of people I know well, I give credence to many of the horror stories circulating on the Internet about various offshore sports books.

Two years ago, a wealthy gambler from California, call him Mr. J, opened an account with one of the largest of the offshore books. This VBO is located in Costa Rica—one of those worrisome jurisdictions where, at present, the "license" a sports book needs is the same general business license granted to, say, a hot-dog vendor. Mr. J deposited $200,000 with which to wager and, over the course of a nine-week period, managed to blow it all. The VBO called him at home and encouraged him to deposit more money, promising that he'd be granted higher limits so that he might have a chance to recoup his losses. Mr. J did just that and, thanks to some excellent advice, allegedly from one of the sharpest sports bettors in America, had two successive winning weeks. Big winning weeks. In fact, the Californian managed to churn his replenished bankroll into $486,000. Now he wanted a payout.

Mr. J never got a penny of his winnings.

What he did get was a promise from the VBO's CEO, a former New York and Miami street bookie, that he would never see his money again. Despite having lost for nine straight weeks, Mr. J, according to the VBO's boss, was betting "steam" games [slang for "smart money"] on the advice of a famous bettor and poker player out of Las Vegas.

In late 2000, another gambler, this one a $100 bettor, hit a long-shot six-team baseball parlay—the kind that comes in about once every two years—and won more than $30,000 from a heavily promoted VBO. For three months, the VBO tried to avoid paying, claiming variously that the gambler had exceeded his betting limits, that their software was faulty, that he had tried to "defraud" the company, ad nauseam. As of this writing, after months of dissembling and wriggling, the VBO has yet to pay the man. The story being circulated on the Internet message boards is that the gambler will be allowed to collect his winnings on the condition that he fly down to Costa Rica (at the book's expense) and not talk to anyone about the "settlement." This wouldn't be such a scary proposition, if not for the fact that the CEO of this particular VBO has a penchant for surrounding himself with armed bodyguards.

I personally experienced the VBO mambo three years ago. Early one week, when the lines were first released, I made several large (for me) wagers on college football games being played on the coming Saturday. All of the games were on television, and I figured the "price" would go up later in the week, primarily since I was betting the favorites, which the mythical "public" seems to support almost every contest. My hypothesis proved correct. Thanks to an avalanche of money on the favorites, the odds did climb, from something like six points to seven or eight.

All three of my favorites won and covered the spread that weekend. And they would have returned a healthy profit. Unfortunately, I never got to cash my tickets— the VBO's owner had unilaterally canceled my wagers the day before the game. He didn't like that the line had moved so far in my favor.

Imagine as a bettor being able to cancel your wager when you find out two hours before game time that the star quarterback you were banking on has broken a bone in his throwing hand while conducting a drug deal with some indigent prostitutes. "Hi, Mr. Bookie, I'm pretty sure my team is going to lose now, so, if you don't mind, I'm going to just call off last Tuesday's bets."

When I discovered my bets had been canceled without my permission, I called down to find out how the VBO could justify such outrageous behavior. According to the CEO, the line moves I benefited from indicated I was obviously some sort of sharp bettor or connected to good information and, therefore, I might not actually lose the majority of my wagers. And that's not the kind of customer they value. So: no bet!

I pointed out to him one of the sacrosanct rules of sports gambling, not to mention contracts in general: Once both parties agree to the wager, the bet stands, unless it is canceled by mutual agreement.

The boss man explained to me that the only "rule" that really counted was that he was holding the money and, therefore, could make up the regulations as he went along. And if I didn't like it, too bad. And if I complained too much, I might never see any of my money again. You got a problem wit dat?

I reluctantly agreed to the cancellation of my wagers and spent five anxious days waiting to see if the money from my closed account would ever arrive back in the United States. (It did, thankfully—minus about $100 for "transaction fees.")

It gets worse.

The most recent stain in the offshore sports book industry's dirty underwear concerns self-proclaimed provisos that blatantly "sanction" the books to keep your money at will.

Several well-known VBOs, some of which have recently enjoyed gushing profiles in large-circulation men's magazines, have allowed themselves a veritable license to steal in the form of "confiscation clauses" buried within their house rules. These provisos are primarily meant to scare away professional bettors, but they can be exercised at the bookie's whim against anyone he chooses to victimize.

Here's one such clause, posted on a Web site under the heading of "fraud."

"Any and all bets placed in an attempt in any way to defraud [VBO] will be deemed void. Any and all bets made or contracted by any professional gambler or member, employee or associate of a professional sports-wagering group, or family member of such a person or group, who has not previously identified themselves to management, shall be voided and the balances in such accounts held by [the VBO]."

Here's another.

"Professional sports gamblers are not allowed membership at [our sports book]. If a suspected professional sports gambler does open an account at [our sports book, we] reserve the right to 1) cancel this account at any time without notice, and 2) refund any initial deposits made by the professional sports gambler into [his betting] account as [our sports book's] only liability towards any and all winnings the professional sports gambler may have achieved."

And here's a third, which I found on one Web site hidden under a link called "Terms and Conditions of Use."

"If we consider you to be a Restricted Individual, you are not permitted to register with us or to access our Wagering Services. If you circumvent our controls and do open an account with us, we reserve the right to 1) cancel your account without notice and 2) void all transactions you have made with us and refund your initial deposit back to you. We consider you a Restricted Individual if you (1) are under 18 years of age (2) reside in Canada or any jurisdiction where Internet gambling is expressly prohibited (3) have been banned for any reason by any government licensed land or Internet-based casino or sports betting facility located anywhere in the world (4) are a bookmaker or an employee of a bookmaker using our Wagering Services in the course of your employment or (5) are a member of any type of professional gambling partnership or syndicate."

It's bad enough that the books operating out of distant Third World offices can keep your money whenever they please, but now you're forced to agree to it beforehand. To play with these shops, you must accept terms that are, in no uncertain terms, unacceptable.

Now, granted, many bookmakers aren't prepared to deal with gamblers who know more about sports betting than they do. Even a number of betting shops on the Don Best Premium feed, an instant odds service that tracks the flow of "smart money" around the world, abhor so-called "wiseguy" business. (The Don Best Premium feed costs $500 a month; what kind of gambler do these bookmakers think they're going to attract? Ten-dollar teaser bettors?)

Nonetheless, none of the reputable wiseguy-phobic outfits, including the brick-and-mortar sports books in Nevada, would ever stoop to a confiscation clause. While most sports books, in Nevada and offshore, will chase away players they believe are sharp, trying instead to build a clientele of total squares with no chance to win, the vast majority of these outfits handle the money honorably. Typically, these books simply pay off sharp winning players, then immediately close their accounts.

But I'm not a professional gambler, you might claim. And you might or might not be. Doesn't matter either way. The books with the provisos can stiff a player and be totally within their rules, so long as they *proclaim* him to be a professional.

This situation is akin to a totalitarian government that prosecutes its citizenry for thinking unpure thoughts. Scared of being brought before a fascist tribunal, the populace learns to keep their thoughts to themselves or, even safer, purge thoughts in general from their mind. Likewise, gamblers who play with shops that have a "professionals-not-allowed" clause become conditioned to lose. For if they pick winners consistently (which is what professional gamblers supposedly do) at a demonstrably higher rate than the 50% clip the average punter manages, they've been forewarned that their money will be confiscated.

Let's forget for a moment that everyone who opens an account with an offshore bookie is trying to win, even if he doesn't necessarily believe it's going to happen; he's still going to try. Let's also conveniently ignore for a moment that everyone who opens an account with an offshore bookie has a reasonable chance to hit a hot streak in which he picks substantially more winners than losers. Let's also set aside the obvious fact that even the dumbest squirrel in the tree occasionally stumbles upon an acorn—which might, for instance, take the form of a long-shot six-team baseball parlay.

The VBO's "professional-gambler" provision allows them to unilaterally decide to keep (steal) your money. It's right there in their rules, and there's not a damn thing you can do about it—is there?

My experience of not getting paid on my winning wagers led me to wonder about the bigger picture. After all, this VBO has been "endorsed" by myriad Web sites and magazines. So I called several of those that had recommended the place so highly, the ones that had promised me that I would be dealing with one of the most reputable and honorable operations in the business. I told them what had happened to me. They made all the appropriate noises—"That's shocking! We'll look into this right away!"—and subsequently did nothing. Well, not exactly nothing. They continued to cheerfully tout this VBO as the best offshore bookmaking operation on the planet.

This puzzled me. I couldn't comprehend how Web sites and publications that were ostensibly "looking out for the players" could know of the VBO's indiscretions, yet still promote the shop. (Yes, I was woefully naive.) Strange, I thought. Maybe I'm the only person ever jerked around by this place.

Then I did a little investigating. I learned I wasn't the only victim. Dozens of people had lodged complaints (on gambler's forums and with the offshore sports betting "watchdog" agencies) about this and other VBOs canceling bets, withholding winnings, and threatening to confiscate accounts if the aggrieved bettor made too much noise.

Still, the "watchdogs" continued to enthusiastically steer gamblers to their portals.

As Boss Tweed once famously said, "It ain't the votes that count. It's the people that do the counting that count." Tammany Hall; Costa Rica — the story's the same.

Turns out—stop me if you've heard this one before—VBOs often pay these (private) organizations to shill for them.

Imagine the magazine *Consumer Reports* being subsidized by Microsoft, Toyota, and Phillip Morris. Were it so, you'd certainly be forgiven for cocking a skeptical eyebrow when the magazine's Products of the Year turned out to be Marlboro cigarettes, Camry sedans, and Windows 2000. In the shadowy world of offshore sports books, this kind of incestuous relationship is depressingly common—only none of the so-called consumer advocates bothers to alert their readers to the arrangement.

Despite their impassioned protestations of innocence, despite the "good deeds" they claim to have performed on behalf of aggrieved gamblers, anything these "watchdogs" say—or endorse, or whatever—should be taken with a heaping handful (forget the grain) of salt. Most of these "watchdogs" shill for dishonorable VBOs, despite being intimately familiar with the book's track record.

I decided to contact one alleged "Offshore Watchdog" (OW) after reviewing its list of endorsed sports books and discovering that it contained two genuine stinkers. I called the 800 number and told the OW that a prominent outfit, one of the shops on their list, had taken six months to pay me one weekend's worth of winnings. After professing their shock at my discouraging news, the OW never did a thing besides equivocate—and they continue to shill for the joint. Which makes perfect sense, since it's highly probable that it helped fund the OW. Far from being "watchdogs," many OWs are merely marketing organizations for the books that pay them.

One sports book manager, whose Curacao-based shop appears on one OW's list, admitted to me that the OW was just another promotional tool for him, a cheap marketing play on a price-versus-appearance basis. But as far as actually being a consumer advocate? He tried to address that question, but he was laughing too hard.

Another of the so-called OWs claims to provide an "open forum" where the free exchange of information and ideas will make the offshore sports-betting world a better and safer place for those who send their money to distant lands. Originally an outlet to sell picks on sporting events, the site's founder discovered that the watchdog business was far more lucrative. After proving to be a below-average game picker and an above-average promoter, the brains behind the site began "covering" (as in journalistically) the offshore bookmaking world—and, incidentally, accepting advertisements from those he was "covering."

As you might surmise, the necessary separation of Church and State, of advertising and editorial, which must exist if a publication intends its critical writing about potential advertisers to be credible, does not exist here. Indeed, one site features comically horrible articles written by someone who works as a paid consultant to the marketing department of a larcenous VBO. Thus, while it's a nice concept in theory, the OWs in practice do not believe in treating advertisers objectively. Their ethos seems to be, "If a sports book pays to appear on my site, their sins, past and present, are automatically absolved— at least until enough people raise a fuss about them." In such cases they tend to remove the offenders for a time, only to reinstate them when the clamor from disgruntled players dies down.

The condition is surprisingly widespread. In fact, even formerly trustworthy OWs become compromised by the incestuous relationship between self-proclaimed lookouts and the sports books who pay their bills. As these Internet watchdogs grow (and attract more advertising money), they inevitably begin to promote several sports books that engage in unsavory practices. Freedom of speech is still tolerated on some of the OW message boards, but the rapidly deteriorating ethical standards of even the best-intentioned OW sites make them better resources for promotion-hungry bookies than concerned gamblers.

This all may seem like much ado about a not-very-clever con. In fact, the equivocations and obfuscations of the OWs are darkly funny to long-time observers. But the uninitiated, who stumble across the various OW Web sites in search of guidance, can be easily misled. The people behind the exceedingly clever (and official-looking) monikers and acronyms that the OWs employ are promoters first and foremost, and their pitches can be compelling.

Which leads to a related question that you may, by now, be asking. Why, the sensible person might justifiably wonder, would anyone in their right mind play with one of these patently bad offshore shops? I mean, trying to win a sports bet at 4.54% the worst of it is difficult enough. Gamblers shouldn't have to worried about getting paid.

One possibility is that longtime customers of certain VBOs that close accounts or confiscate funds may have been (accurately) pegged as stone cold idiots. Otherwise, they'd have been asked to leave a long time ago. In reality, the average gambler wins some and loses some, and never accumulates enough net winnings, even if running lucky, to draw attention to his account. Hence, the relationship survives. If the bettor is going to lose anyway, it will never really matter that he's dealing with a suspect book. But if fortune happens to smile too widely, watch out!

Why do sensible people sign up with bad bookies in the first place? Usually it's because someone trustworthy told them to. Someone—or something, like a full-page ad in a national magazine—told the unsuspecting gambler that there was nothing to worry about. Someone steered an ignorant player in the wrong direction, all the while assuring him (and thousands of others) that he was making a sound decision. Like Jim Jones leading his followers into the Guyana jungle, where deadly Kool-Aid awaited them, these authoritative voices knowingly lead legions of pigeons to the slaughterhouse.

Don't be lulled by slick presentations. One great advantage enjoyed by the VBOs is their VBBs—as in Very Big Bankrolls. Those bankrolls often pay for expensive ads and beautiful four-color brochures. Some of these VBOs delight in repeatedly reminding you of their greatness through enough direct-mail campaigns to wipe out an entire old-growth forest. Once you get on their mailing list, you can look forward to weekly greetings from your would-be best buddies in Central America. Every other time you open your mailbox, you'll find it stuffed

with flashily produced testimonials, glowingly reminding you that this or that VBO is the world's biggest and
best sports book.

As I write this report, the mailman has arrived with
the day's delivery. For the second time this month, I've
gotten junk mail from a VBO. Adding insult to injury,
it's the same one that unceremoniously showed me the
door just months ago. (But they sure do have nice-look-
ing half-naked ladies on their advertisements, and the
fruit baskets they send out at Christmas are awful swell.)

So then, where is it safe to play?

The answer depends on what kind of gambler you
are. As alluded to earlier, if you're a casual bettor, a "leisure" player as the bookies say, you're going to lose most
(if not all) of your bankroll anyway if you play long
enough. But you at least want the pleasure of the occasional hot streak before your inevitable demise. So it's
fundamental that you avoid the notorious sports books
that are basically elaborate excuses for credit-card fraud.
These con artists will rob you of your money, not to mention your fleeting pleasure. A comprehensive list of such
miscreants can be found in a diligent Internet search.

So much for the outright thieves, liars, and cheats.
There are hundreds of bookmakers offshore who won't
steal, won't cheat, and won't threaten. Your money is
probably as secure with them as any FDIC-insured bank.
That's the good news. The bad news is I can't recommend playing with them either. If you're a "serious"
player—that is to say you do research and shop for good
numbers and manage your money responsibly—you
probably bet more than the chronic loser and, at the end
of the season, might even show a profit for your troubles.
In other words, you're good, which means many offshore
bookies don't want your business. These guys are known
as "shoemakers" or "dressmakers," bookies who will
only court your action if they're certain you'll lose. Much

like casinos that bar card counters from their blackjack games, these bookmakers/shoemakers aren't clever enough to handle so-called "smart" action; they resent that some gamblers know more about betting sports than the average bookie does, and they do everything in their power to chase away anyone but bona fide buffoons. And when they do, you can forget about that nice 10%-20% deposit bonus you were counting on; that's only for "good" (read: "losing") customers.

These losers-only joints, also known colloquially as "clones," since they primarily follow the line moves of the bigger and more expert shops, do not rob their customers. In fact, most of them have impeccable reputations for paying. If you're a sharp player, however, they will make it eminently clear in a panoply of ways that your business is not appreciated.

Many of these clone joints don't necessarily want to book bets, anyway. They want to either bet on the games themselves with other bookies or guess at the "hot" sides favored by wiseguy betting syndicates. A startling number of offshore shops move their pointspreads up and down without ever taking a wager, thereby forfeiting the magic "juice" that, over the long run, makes most bookies very wealthy fellows. Then they wonder why the sharps beat them and the squares stay away.

One of the surest ways to dissuade action (and, when it happens, an easy way for bettors to identify a churn joint) is to stall a customer on the phone, making him wait interminably while the line moves. Imagine discovering that a company whose stock you own is going to announce that their eagerly awaited wonder drug has been shown in clinical tests to cause mice to grow an extra tail. You call your broker to dump your stock. His secretary puts you on hold for ten minutes while the price plunges.

This goes on almost daily at many offshore shops. News leaks out of a key injury in the Pistons-Lakers game.

You call up to make a bet before ESPN breaks the story on SportsCenter. Now, if the bookie has noticed that the line tends to move after you make your bets, you can count on him employing the old four-corner offense. (Remember, this is a putatively honest bookie that pays, so you're still making bets with him, even as he discourages your business.)

In an article on the sports gambling Web site *The Daily Spread*, Heath Bouthwell accurately described what happens next:

> *You've never seen such a chronic outbreak of amnesia and blindness in all your life:*
>
> *Once they get your pin number, these seemingly educated, nimble, English-speaking, able-bodied, healthy clerks no longer "habla ingles," — or they can't see the board, or they drop the phone, or whatever their routine of the moment is to lay down a stall.*
>
> *Note: The quicker you ask for the game, the longer it takes them to enunciate their syllables. The really good/experienced clerks will respond with something like this.*
>
> *"Okaaayyyy siiirrr, leeetttt mmmmmeeeeee seeeeeeeeeee ... thaaaaaaaattttttsssss" (sounds of mindless clatter in the background as clerk feigns an attempt to pull the game up on his terminal) "gaaaaaaaaaaaammmmmmmeeeeeeee nuummmbeeer" (more clatter; his damn arthritis must be acting up, poor guy) "706/707, riiiiiiiiiigggggghhhhhhhttt???? Okaayyyy, leeeeettss seeeeeee thhhhheeeeee ..."*
>
> *Boom! The line starts to change everywhere and they snap out of their trance and start spitting out well formed sentences faster than that guy in the FedEx commercial:*
>
> *"The Pistons are six and eighty-four, sir!"*
>
> *They proclaim this proudly—as if they had the line*

there all along, but just couldn't quite find it. And once they did finally "locate" it, boy, they've got a crucial obligation to deliver it to you in a hurry! Can't keep the customer waiting!

Because I know some of the top gamblers in the world and am privy to their advice and wisdom on betting sports, I have been booted, chased, and harangued for winning, playing "steam," being "too smart," and generally not being "the kind of customer we're looking for." Because I've done my homework and have for years paid very close attention to all matters concerning Internet bookmaking and betting, I've formed conclusions as to which shops are likely to adhere to the highest overall standards of forthrightness and honor.

Conversely, I have informed opinions about shops that do not meet what I consider high standards. There are, I'm afraid, hundreds of this ilk, many of which you'll never encounter—too many, in fact, to list here. The higher-profile shops that fall under the heading "Places I Wouldn't Send a Friend" appear below:

All World	Jaguar
Betmaker.com	Millennium
Bowman's	NASA International
Darwin All Sports	SBG Global
Diamond International	SOS
First Fidelity Deposit	SportingbetUSA
Gameday	Sportbet.com
Horizon	Sportsbetting.com
Infinity	VIP Sports
International Island	William Hill
Intertops	

You may not find these sports books on any sort of warning list, because most of them don't ostensibly do anything "wrong"—such as abscond with your deposit. Be aware, however, that these shops are meant for losers only; i.e., if you play with these shops you are probably a loser, since long-term winners are usually shown the door.

To be fair, no bookmaker is in business to lose, and the onshore sports books of Las Vegas are often no better than their expatriate brethren. The Las Vegas Hilton Superbook, an enormous operation housed in a casino the size of an airplane hangar, is notorious for chasing out anyone they suspect has a chance of winning, and some of the newer megaresorts, like the Venetian, impose betting limits worthy of a barroom bookie working out of Alaquippa, Pennsylvania. But there's one compelling difference between the ons and the offs: No matter how bad the customer service, no matter how weak the lines, the Vegas bookies are regulated and accountable.

But we can't all get to Las Vegas whenever we want to make a bet.

So what's the avid sports gambler to do? In a phrase: Be skeptical, be cautious, and don't believe the hype.

Despite the unsavory picture I've generally painted about the offshore books, I can recommend several operations wholeheartedly. If the majority of bookmakers conducted their business with the integrity and fairness that the following outfits consistently do, I would feel confident endorsing the offshore-sports-book industry as a whole. Up until now, at least, these elite few have been demonstrated to be safe, secure, smart shops that aren't afraid to take a bet. The following are the places that I would recommend to friends, the ones I think deserve your business.

SportsMarket: One of the last of the "old-time" bookmakers, SportsMarket realizes the key to being a successful bookie is writing tickets. Square, sharp—doesn't matter. If you're willing to lay them 11-10, they'll gladly (and professionally) book your wager. My personal favorite. Based in Curacao.

W.I.T. Sports: The acronym stands for "Whatever It Takes," and this shop, whose line manager was the long-time boss at the sports book at Caesars Palace in Las Vegas, bends over backwards to provide first-class customer service, interesting lines, and accommodating limits. Winners here are paid with a smile. Based in Costa Rica.

CRIS/ABC Islands: A huge operation known for booking the world's biggest and sharpest sports bettors. Most of the smaller shops imitate their lines, which are considered sharper than the lines out of Vegas. As solid as the industry gets. Based in Costa Rica.

WWTS: One of the pioneering offshore books famed for financial stability, fair business practices, and good customer service. This book is run like a small corporation, not some backroom sweatshop. Offers high limits and an even higher degree of trustworthiness. Based in Antigua.

Olympic Sports: Virtually every offshore wannabe bookie follows the line moves at this industry leader. Known for an enormous array of betting lines, this shop is both financially stable and fun to play with. Based in Jamaica.

Canbet: Licensed and bonded in Australia, where bookmaking has been legal for more than a century, Canbet books all the major American sports, as well as most of the favorite "international" matches. (Cricket, anyone?) Their Internet software is easy to use and, best of all, they charge only 7% juice (-107) on most straight bets.

The Luckiest Man In The World

John Brinson is surely the luckiest man in the world.

Brinson, 46, a retired U.S. Army veteran living in Goldsboro, North Carolina, was picked at random from some three million entries to attempt the "Gillette Three-Point Challenge," a made-for-television publicity stunt conducted during the 1997 NCAA Final Four. This is the deal: Make a basketball shot from behind the college three-point line and Gillette's insurance company pays out $1 million over 20 years; miss and Gillette provides a $50,000 consolation prize. Either scenario translates into a tasty windfall for the contestant.

How tasty? Given that Mr. Brinson can make three-pointers about 25% of the time he tries, the "expected value"—as mathematicians and gamblers like to say—of his Three-Point Challenge is $287,500. ($1 million one-out-four times plus $50,000 the other three times equals $1,150,000; divided by four.) Remember, this gift was bestowed upon him when his name was picked from approximately three million other entries. If you want a sense of how daunting such odds are, see how long it takes you to count to three million. (Go really fast and it shouldn't take more than a year.) Like I said, John Brinson is a very lucky man.

He'll tell you as much. "Oh, I'm very lucky. Always been my whole life," he reports, chatting in an Indianapolis hotel lobby the evening before his date with the three-point line. "I mean, just surviving Vietnam, when I saw so many of my friends never come back. And the time I was in a car accident in Tennessee. I was rear-ended by a drunk driver. Should have been in critical condition, or worse. But I walked away. I *know* I'm lucky."

But no amount of luck, or good fortune, or anything short of divine intervention can explain John Brinson being selected to shoot a three-point basket at the 1997 Final Four.

Because two years earlier, in a similar contest, John Brinson was selected from more than one million entries to attempt a $1 million 10-foot putt. (He missed.)

The odds of one person being picked for both events, according to Dr. Cris Poor, a mathematics professor at Fordham University, are more than a trillion to one. That's twelve zeroes: 1,000,000,000,000-to-1. In other words, odds that are not merely once in a lifetime, but more like once in the history of civilization.

Being the man who for many years created the "Vegas line," the betting odds for every major (and minor) sporting event in the world, including the World Series, the Super Bowl, and the Stanley Cup, Michael "Roxy" Roxborough knows a little something about odds. I ask Roxy about John Brinson's incredible luck. "The sun is a bigger favorite to blow up tomorrow than something like this to happen," Roxy says. "There's no mathematical equivalent I could even give you, it's so ridiculous. I would have a better chance of scoring back-to-back one-night-stands with Sharon Stone and Cindy Crawford."

So Brinson getting picked at random twice from millions of entries is impossible? "It's not impossible," Roxy concedes. "But let's put it this way: There's definitely something fishy. I'm not saying there was fraud, but I will say whoever conducted the draw has lost a lot of credibility."

Purely from an oddsmaker's point of view, Brinson's luck is unfathomable. Living in Vegas for many years, Roxy believes in probabilities, not miracles.

He may have a point.

I've seen a videotape of the Gillette drawing, held in what looks to be a warehouse. On it, a lady with a Midwestern accent narrates while another lady in a green dress makes the selections. First you see four huge 1,000-pound-capacity boxes of mail, each filled, according to the narrator, with trays of mail-in entries. (You can't see inside the boxes.) The narrator says that they have drawn a numbered ping-pong ball at random to select which box the winner will come from. (You don't see this part.) Then the tape cuts to a shot of six trays of mail, each holding several hundred entries inside their original envelopes, spread across the floor. The narrator says they will now select a numbered ping-pong ball to determine which tray the winner will come from. The on-camera lady in green reaches into an uncovered plastic bowl, swishes around what one presumes are several balls (you can't see this part clearly), and plucks out a ball with a "1" drawn on it. She then walks to the first tray, looks directly at the envelopes, riffles through them as if locating an alphabetically arranged file, and pulls out an envelope. She cuts it open and reads the winner's name from what one presumes is an entry slip. (You can't see the writing clearly.)

It's John David Brinson.

If any Las Vegas casino conducted its keno games in this sloppy fashion, the Gaming Control Board would have it shut down in ten minutes.

But what motive would anyone have to rig the draw?

Admittedly, John Brinson is a public-relations dream-come-true. Vietnam vet, certified foster parent, pledged to invest his winnings on a local youth center—this is the kind of solid citizen you can root for, the kind of Everyman hero with whom a jillion-dollar corporation would like to be associated.

Whether putting, or shooting a three-pointer, or pitching a baseball into a small net, average Joes and Janes plucked from obscurity have a reasonable opportunity to fulfill that insistent American dream: to get rich overnight. Tapping into our fondness for fairy tales in which an anonymous underdog does something wonderful and transformational, these million-dollar challenges, which Gillette invented and others have since copied, are enormously powerful—and cost-effective—marketing tools. Eric Kraus, the director of communications for Gillette, tells me, "Our million-dollar promotions have been excellent. They're exciting, highly visible and, ultimately, they help move a lot of product. They're great for our retailers, great for our consumers, and great for our company. It's a chance for us to create what we call a 'mega-moment.' It's a fabulous promotion."

Though Kraus won't divulge precise figures, he acknowledges that the premiums his company pays for insurance in the event someone wins—at the time of Brinson's three-pointer-for-cash the public was 0-for-9 in Gillette-sponsored contests—is less than 10% of the total prize.

"Actually, it costs us more if the contestant misses," Kraus reports. "We have to pay the consolation prize." Even worse, his company doesn't get millions of dollars in free publicity from the "mega-moment" being replayed on countless local news broadcasts and sports highlight shows, as Hershey's did when one of its contest winners kicked a million-dollar field goal. "Believe me, we want John to win," Kraus says. "We're rooting for him."

How hard? I wonder. Badly enough to cook the results of a random draw? Tempting, but unlikely. Because while the possibility of corporate chicanery may be there, Brinson's badly conducted selection was probably less about a rigged draw than it was about miracles. Screwball comedy miracles. Guardian angels. Good things happening to good guys.

The night before John Brinson will have his second chance at winning $1 million, I ask him if he thinks his selection was indeed a miracle. "I believe we all get blessings every day. They come in different forms. This wasn't a miracle. This was a blessing. But you know," he says, smiling warmly, "I feel like I'm blessed whether I win a million dollars or not. Every day I feel that way."

I ask him if he's suffering from the unavoidable stress and strain of performing a life-altering feat on live television, before a worldwide audience. "Nah," he says nonchalantly, almost sincerely enough that you believe him. "I'm more excited about the North Carolina basketball game than I am about the shot. See, I'm very positive. If I make it, I'll be *rich* and positive. You know, with my military background—the discipline, the rigorous training—shooting a basket isn't anything to worry about."

Brinson's wife, Margaret, concurs. "I'm not nervous. He's going to make it. I know he is."

"Oh, yeah, it's going in," John says. "I'm going to make it. I feel it. I dream about it. I see it going in. And after I make it, or even if I don't, I'm just going to go home and harvest my potatoes and my greens."

Brinson has reason to feel confident. For the past eight months he's submitted to a regimen of daily practice—at least an hour or two a day—shooting 19'9" baskets until his "stroke" is as smooth and repeatable as Reggie

Miller's. Twice he's consorted with NBA Hall of Famer Rick Barry, a celebrity coach hired by Gillette, to work on technique. Brinson's practice sessions, at the local YMCA back home, attract an enthusiastic audience, many of whom offer the world's luckiest man advice, secrets, and good wishes for his (second) shot-of-a-lifetime. He says he's been averaging between 20% and 30% success.

Based on those numbers, I suggest to Brinson that his shot is actually more likely to miss than make. On the other hand, if luck comes into play …

"I know it's going in," he says. "I want the ball to bounce around on the rim a little bit, keep everybody in suspense. And all the time I know it's going in."

Margaret Brinson shakes her head in disbelief at her man's sense of drama, and takes her husband off to bed.

The next morning, the morning of The Shot, in a limousine on the way to a live segment for the "Today" show, John Brinson tells me he slept perfectly. And he looks it. The man is loose, with an equanimity befitting a Buddhist monk. "I feel like a million," he says, beaming.

During warm-ups for his television spot, the Million Dollar Man sinks seven three-pointers in a row. On camera, he misses his first two attempts and sinks the third. The stroke looks good.

"He's been making about thirty percent," Rick Barry tells me. "I'm just hoping when he's shooting for the money it'll be one of the good three. If luck has anything to do with it, we know that part is on his side."

Though Barry believes shooting underhanded is the softest and most efficient way to make the big basket, he chose not to change Brinson's natural overhand shot. "He's a big strong guy," Barry says. "I've just been stressing to him: Shoot it high; use your legs! Legs and up! Legs and up! People miss because they shoot the ball flat. Legs and up!"

Brinson nods at his teacher. "Legs and up. Right."

Imagine what it must be like to know you will (or won't) win a million dollars by the end of the day. What do you do? What do you think about? For the six hours prior to showtime, John Brinson spends a quiet day back at his hotel. He reads the paper and the Bible, naps, watches C-SPAN, calls home, thinks. "And I saw Kareem in the lobby, carrying his own luggage: Exciting!"

Only hours before his test, I ask him the great sports-caster cliche question: How do you feel?

"I'm ready," he replies. "Very ready."

"We don't need any more time," Margaret Brinson says, sighing. She wants to get it over with, like a prisoner facing the executioner. "We're ready."

We ride to the Hinkle Fieldhouse at Butler University, a gorgeous old gym where the basketball movie *Hoosiers* was filmed. Thanks to the supposed sanctity of college athletics, that great bastion of scholar-mercenaries, Gillette cannot conduct its publicity stunt at the RCA Dome, site of the Final Four, since the NCAA does not allow the stain of sponsor money to taint the virgin purity of their amateur tournament. No signs allowed in the arena! This from an organization that takes in hundreds of millions of dollars every year, mostly in CBS television rights and the rest in ticket sales and over-priced souvenirs.

The gym is packed with Indiana basketball fans, lured to the event by free pizza and plenty of Gillette-related gifts. When he's introduced to the roaring crowd, John Brinson smiles warmly, but you can tell his blood has turned to ice. The portent of the moment has hit him, and no amount of blessings will put the basketball through the hoop. Only he can do that now.

Brinson retires to an auxiliary court to warm up. This is not a problem: Within five minutes of practice shots, he hands Margaret his nylon jacket; it's soaking wet. Even more ominous foreshadowing follows: As Rick Barry urges him on with exhortations of "Legs and up!" John Brinson makes about one shot in 20. (I help scurry after the elusive rebounds.)

When an announcer calls out the two-minute-warning—"Two minutes to live national television!"— Brinson's right hand goes to his chin, in a pensive repose. Who knows what he's thinking? I'm too scared to open my mouth and ask.

Then, after a brief on-camera interview, with the crowd in a frenzy, John Brinson takes his million-dollar shot.

About halfway to the basket you can tell the ball isn't going in. Brinson pulls his attempt to the left—as he did his putt—missing the rim. It's a brick. John smiles graciously, but for a moment there is collective heartbreak in that Indianapolis gym. I feel like I'm going to cry— and then I realize I've been holding my breath since Brinson stepped to the line.

Rick Barry is disappointed. "He never got the legs into it. Never had a chance." Eric Kraus, the Gillette official, is disappointed. "We can't *buy* a winner! If we had a winner, they'd lose the check." I'm disappointed.

The only one who isn't disappointed is John Brinson. "You have no idea how fun that was," he tells me. "This was a lot better than the putt. When I missed it the crowd wasn't loud. This time it was *loud*, like they were all my family." Brinson turns to a downcast congregation of Gillette functionaries, all of whom are doing a not very good job of keeping a stiff upper lip.

"Don't worry, guys," says the luckiest man in the world, for whom trillion-to-one odds are merely numbers on a sheet of paper. He flashes a consoling smile at his sponsors. "It's all right. I'll see you next year."

The Line Mover 7

You're in Las Vegas. You've got money in your pocket. And you've got a strong opinion on the "Monday Night Football" match-up.

You wander into a sports book, where virtually every athletic contest in America has a price on it. You scan the boards, skipping over college football and a World Series game, searching for tonight's NFL line.

There it is: The Giants are favored by 13^1/$_2$ points over the Bears. You like the Giants, playing at home. However, even though you're certain the Giants will win the game, 13^1/$_2$ points seems like a lot to spot the Bears. That's almost two touchdowns, you think, fingering the money in your pocket. You hesitate, weighing the pros and cons. *Can the Giants win by two touchdowns? Well, on paper New York should dominate. ... Of course, Chicago might get a lucky last-minute break. ... On the other hand, the Giants usually play well at home on Monday night. ... Hmmm.*

Finally, you convince yourself the Giants are a good bet at 13^1/$_2$. You approach the window, minutes before the kick-off, ready to slide your stack of hundreds across the counter.

And then it happens: The 13^1/$_2$ changes to 14^1/$_2$.

"Wait a minute," you tell the clerk. "I wanted to bet the Giants at thirteen and a half."

"Too late," he says, shrugging. "The line just moved. Should have bet five minutes ago."

Indeed. Now the Giants don't look so attractive. Now they have to win by *more than* two touchdowns. Now you might even bet the Bears.

"What happened?" you ask the clerk. "What happened to the odds?"

"Sir," the clerk says, smiling, "you just got stung by the Line Mover."

Welcome to the club.

The Line Mover is the most powerful—and successful—bettor in all of sports. He and his organization, a syndicate of approximately two dozen well-capitalized gamblers, exert the kind of influence over America's sports betting odds that, were it occurring on Wall Street, would be called manipulating the market. Regularly wagering as much as $500,000 per football game, the Line Mover inspires fear in bookmakers, confusion in those who would try to piggy-back on his expertise, and hope in millions of casual sports bettors around the world who would like to think that there's someone out there who really can consistently beat the game.

Speaking on the condition of anonymity, the Line Mover sat down with me and revealed how America's biggest sports betting syndicate operates.

"It's pretty simple," he says flatly. "We find situations where we have way the best of it, and then we bet a whole lot of money. Do that enough and you end up with a nice little profit."

How nice? He won't say exactly. But the Line Mover does volunteer that over the past five years he has paid on average $3 million in taxes on his winnings. "We do pretty well," he deadpans, nodding contentedly.

Of the Line Mover, Michael "Roxy" Roxborough, who for many years ran the company that produces the Las Vegas line, says, "Anybody can walk into a Nevada sports book and bet on a game. The truth is, we don't worry about the average gambler. We worry about [the Line Mover]. There's only four or five guys we're really concerned about. We design the line with these guys in mind. Sports betting is a game of skill. Give a really skill-ful sports bettor a big bankroll and he's dangerous. A guy like [the Line Mover] is the reason we have limits. He's the reason we have to be so careful."

Of Roxy Roxborough, the man who spends each working day trying to take his money, the Line Mover says, "The man has a very difficult job. He's trying to make a line for the casinos to get two-sided action [equal bets on both teams], and he does a good job at that. But he can't keep up with me, because I'm the tenth of one percent that consistently wins. If Roxy ever does catch up, I'll quit tomorrow. In the meantime, even though I think Roxy is a good and admirable opponent, I know I'm going to beat him year in and year out."

America's biggest sports bettor accomplishes this feat by identifying games where the line is "off," or, by his calculations, slightly mistaken. By his reckoning, a foot-ball line that is incorrect by a half point gives him close to a 7% advantage, depending on the number in ques-tion. A line that's off by three points—well, that's a mon-strous edge. The trick, of course, is finding games in which the Las Vegas line is wrong.

Enter the computers. The Line Mover is famous in the gambling world for using up to a half-dozen sophis-ticated computer programs, custom-designed to evalu-ate past performance and predict future results. He won't say what the computers are searching for—"That would be like the magician telling you how he cuts the girl in half," he jokes—but he does reveal that the criteria, when processed properly, yield a chillingly accurate "power rating" that reduces every college and NFL football team to a quantifiable number. Employing a full-time team of handicappers, statistics-obsessed computer junkies who generate a series of daily reports, the Line Mover considers his analysts' data and decides where his organization's money will be invested. "My talent isn't handicapping the games," he admits. "My expertise is handicapping the handicappers—and knowing the best time to bet."

The Line Mover's sense of timing, his nearly extrasensory understanding of how—and *when*—the public will bet a sporting contest, is perhaps his greatest attribute. "I can't emphasize how important timing is in my business. A half-point either way can make or break my profit. So some games we'll bet early Monday morning, some five minutes before the kick-off. All depends what kind of price we think we can get."

Casino sports books constantly adjust their lines based on the amount of money coming in. If, for example, everyone in Nevada seems to be favoring the Giants, the price on them will go up, making a bet on their counterpart, the Bears, more attractive. By offering odds that encourage two-way betting, the bookmakers can keep their accounts fairly balanced, avoiding big swings and virtually guaranteeing a profit. (Since the bookies charge $11 to win $10, $1 million bet on both sides of a game ensures them a $50,000 profit.) When the Line Mover makes his plays, an enormous amount of money comes in on one side, so the bookmakers quickly change their odds to dissuade other gamblers from taking the heavily bet side and encourage them to wager on the lightly bet side. The trick for the Line Mover is to get his money down *before* the bookmakers adjust their lines.

Every time the Line Mover bets a game, hundreds of bettors try to jump on his action. If "the middlers," as the Line Mover calls them, get their bets down at various casinos before the Line Mover does, the odds change, fluctuating by the precious half-point (or more) that makes or breaks his profit.

Also, since no single casino will accept the $250,000-and-up bets that the Line Mover makes, in order to get all their money in play, he and his people are forced to make dozens of smaller bets with dozens of bookies around the world.

This is a sore subject with the Line Mover. He denies that he and his organization bet with illegal bookies, but knowledgeable sources say that the Line Mover would be incapable of plying his trade if he didn't use bookies in, for instance, Dallas, Atlanta, New York, and Chicago. "Try betting three hundred thousand on a regular-season college football game," one professional sports bettor explains. "The local casinos here in Vegas just aren't going to fade [take] that kind of action. And even if they would, you could never get a fair price. By the time you bet your first fifty-thousand, they would start moving the line on you."

Thus, a typical play by the Line Mover works like this. He and his analysts find a game that's "off." Using a pre-determined formula—a half-point warrants a $50,000 bet, two points warrant $250,000, and in rare cases, some lines inspire bets of $1 million—the Line Mover selects his best plays of the day. Some weekends he'll bet as many as 25 college and NFL games; sometimes he'll only bet a handful. "I gamble for value, not action," he says. "I bet by a strict formula. So there's no 'get-even' or 'get-rich' bets. If the numbers don't look good, I pass."

After deciding which contests his organization will bet on, the Line Mover sends out instructions to his associates, via a numerical pager. When the signal goes out to make a play, the Line Mover's team members attempt to make their bet immediately and simultaneously, before the illegal bookies and legal Nevada sports books can adjust their lines unfavorably. Smart bookmakers, recognizing the source of the large bets, often bet with the Line Mover, "laying off" or hedging their money with another, unsuspecting, bookmaker. (Others merely try to avoid taking his bets.) Within minutes, bookmakers in every region of America—and often offshore—are flooded with fresh money, all on one team. Within a few more minutes, the official Las Vegas line moves to reflect the imbalance.

That's why they call him the Line Mover.

He wasn't always the king of the sports bettors. The man who is now widely regarded as one of the most powerful forces in all of gambling was, twenty years ago, indistinguishable from thousands of other wishful thinkers. "I bet on everything at the start and, like everybody else, I lost," the Line Mover remembers. A successful businessman with a chain of appliance stores throughout the Midwest, the Line Mover blew off hundreds of thousands of dollars to local bookies. "It took me a long time to figure out that just reading the morning sports paper wouldn't cut it. Just studying the box scores doesn't work." Instead, he sought out the best minds in the game, the brilliant computer programmers and data analysts who would revolutionize the way we bet on sports. He made them a deal: You provide me with the best information and I'll provide you with the money to do something with it. "And that's how our team was born."

While the Line Mover professes to still love sports, he says, "If my life depended on it, I couldn't tell you who's leading the divisions. I don't even look at the sports pages much. I'm a money manager, not an action-hungry sports fan. Your average sports bettor reads something in the paper or hears something on television and figures he's got some kind of insider information."

Indeed, the professional touts, so-called "experts" who sell their opinions to gullible gamblers via expensive 900 lines, help the Line Mover win his yearly millions. "People follow these touts blindly, like they're in a cult. Ninety percent of the time I bet against the tout's opinion. See, by promoting one side of a game so vigorously, they can sometimes move the line four, five, six points. That," he says, smiling broadly, "tends to create some very profitable situations."

The Super Bowl, according to the Line Mover, is a prime example. For five of the past six years, he says, the line has been dramatically off. Wildly off. "Only problem is, the public's been right. I've bet on every loser."

He says this with a grin, looking very much like a man who is used to being right far more often than he is wrong, a man who can afford to lose a sports bet now and again—a man who is accustomed to knowing before the rest of the world which way the line is going to move.

Blackjack Ball

If you're under the mistaken impression that the gambling industry loves all patrons equally, making no distinction between hopeless suckers and expert winners, consider what might happen if the management of the world's biggest casinos knew the date and location of Max Rubin's annual Blackjack Ball.

"A nice little Scud missile aimed at that party would wipe out a lot of our problems," one casino executive confesses. "In five minutes we could get rid of most of the guys we don't want in our joint."

This executive is joking, of course. To prohibit (or strongly dissuade) the world's best card counters, shuffle trackers, and other expert advantage players, many of whom attend the Blackjack Ball, casinos don't have to resort to finely targeted terrorist attacks. Or even random murders. By law, they may simply "bar" the customers they don't care to serve.

But the threat of being charged with criminal trespass usually does not deter serious blackjack professionals. A change of name, a different look (sometimes by disguise), and they're back in business. No matter how many detectives from the Griffin Agency (a firm specializing in game security) roam casino floors searching for sophisticated players, the most successful blackjack practitioners will find a way to escape the surveillance net and extract hundreds of thousands of dollars from the gambling industry. Which is why precise directions to the Blackjack Ball are of more than passing interest to the people who run the casinos.

I'm not telling. But I will say this: The Blackjack Ball takes place somewhere in suburban Las Vegas; it's held during a time of year when all of the world's major blackjack teams have players in town; and the guest list includes the greatest collection of gambling talent on the planet, including most of the members of the famed Hyland team (as in "Tommy Hyland," ringleader of America's biggest and best organized blackjack syndicate) and MIT crew (as in "Massachusetts Institute of Technology," from where the three dozen or so teammates earned degrees in math and computer science). The Ball also attracts an equal number of soloists, whose names would mean nothing to the average gambler, but are legendary to those who make a living in the casinos.

According to the Blackjack Ball's popular host, Max Rubin, the *nom de plume* of the garrulous professional gambler who authored the wickedly revealing *Comp City*, getting an invitation requires a personal background check and a previous participant to personally vouch for the newcomer's integrity. Each year about 70 people qualify. If it all sounds vaguely Mafia-like, akin to being a "made" man, there's a reason: One "rat" and the best blackjack players in the world would be instantly out of business.

"If a Griffin [agent] could infiltrate this party," Rubin says, chortling, "it would make the guy's career."

Think of it this way: As a group, the guests at Rubin's Blackjack Ball easily earn at least $5 million a year playing blackjack. Assume that one Las Vegas casino is a particularly easy target and therefore absorbs the brunt of the financial assault. Given that most gaming stocks trade at approximately 15-times earnings, Blackjack Ball guests could costs the casino's parent company up to $75 million in stock value.

The Blackjack Ball started some years ago as a lark, a semi-annual party that was part lodge meeting, part secret society. Most times, whenever the big teams converged in Las Vegas, often at the opening of a new Strip megaresort, 20 to 30 players would informally congregate in a sprawling hotel suite to trade stories, money, and insider information. And while the get-togethers were primarily social, according to Max Rubin the early incarnations of what would eventually grow into the Ball always had an undercurrent of professional pride. To succeed as a gambler, a profession that produces exponentially more losers than winners, demands not only tremendous talent, but a prodigious ego, as well. One does not achieve long-term gambling success of any sort without an enormous belief in one's odds-defying excellence. "If you're making a quarter-million a year playing blackjack, you tend to think you're the best hustler to ever step foot in a casino," Rubin explains.

"At the early parties, guys would be off in a corner, seeing who could count down a deck fastest," Rubin recalls. "And who could cut most accurately, and all the other things blackjack players do. I decided to make it into an organized event."

So while there's much imbibing and story-telling and merry-making in general, the Blackjack Ball these days is primarily a competition, an evening-long test of knowledge and skill that's meant to identify the best blackjack player among the best of blackjack players. Picture a series of friendly bar bets in which all the participants happen to be expert con artists trying to outsmart every other grifter in the joint. It's a swell party.

Max Rubin sees to that. In addition to providing a secure safehouse and a sumptuous buffet, the King of Comps is also the Master of Ceremonies, the Head Adjudicator, and the Grand Quiz Master. In other words, it's Max's party and he makes the rules.

The most peculiar of these is the one that goes something like this: To gain admittance to the Ball, each guest must pay an entry fee of one bottle of champagne produced solely from a casino comp (some participants bring their bubbly with the room service linen still demurely wrapped around the bottle). Furthermore, each guest must bet at least $20 in the Blackjack Ball pari-mutuel betting pool.

"You gotta make 'em," Rubin quips, "'cause most of these guys won't bet on anything where they don't have an edge."

Upon entering the spectacular Rubin estate, an adult playground with the kind of outdoor recreational facilities one normally finds at the better beach resorts, the first thing a visitor sees is a handwritten tote board. But at the Blackjack Ball, instead of horses, the entrants in the race are the guests themselves, whose odds of winning the championship are listed in ascending order. For the 1999 gala, top "ponies" going off at short odds include Arnold Snyder, the publisher of *Blackjack Forum*; Anthony Curtis, the publisher of *Las Vegas Advisor* and a former professional player; J. Chang, the 1998 champion; and several other luminaries who prefer not to see their names in print.

The winner gets a sparkling trophy known as the

Blackjack Cup, the grudging admiration of his peers, and the unofficial title of "Most Feared Man in the Casino Business."

*   *   *

In any setting other than a blackjack pit, most people would not be afraid of the 1999 Champion, "Terry," one of the MIT boys. With thinning hair, extra-thick eyeglasses, and the pasty complexion of someone who spends far too much time indoors, Terry's not an intimidating presence. But put a stack of chips and a deck of cards before him and he's like Kasparov at a chess table. He's transformed from nebbish into trained killer.

Indeed, most of the participants at the Ball are generally unprepossessing men and women, the kind of people whose job demands that they learn to successfully blend into a crowd, keeping their true talents secret from all but their closest colleagues. An outsider would not gaze upon one of the world's best blackjack players and think, "That guy has blackjack expert written all over him." He would think, "Nothing particularly remarkable." A guest at Rubin's Blackjack Ball could easily be your neighbor or your attorney or your friend from the gym.

But there is nothing average about this group. The intelligence quotient in this congregation of professional gamblers is preposterously high, especially when it comes to problem solving. There aren't many other parties in Las Vegas where almost 5% of the guests scored perfect 800s on the mathematics portion of the S.A.T.

*   *   *

After the players spend an hour or two to trade war stories, exchange money ($50,000 bridge loans made on a handshake are not unusual here), and read about themselves in the latest editions of the Griffin book—"Man, that is one ugly mug shot they've got of me!" one well-known counter exclaims—Max Rubin gets on a wireless microphone and calls the congregation to order. "Welcome to the Third Annual Blackjack Ball," he announces. "May everyone I bet on win."

Each participant completes a 20-question preliminary test, meant to weed out the merely very good from the great. [See "The Test."] This is a mix of gambling trivia, rudimentary statistics, and general knowledge. Rubin includes this test, he claims, because a world-class blackjack player should "know about lots of stuff. You never know when it might come in handy."

The 15 top scorers enter the semifinals, where Rubin administers an even more difficult 15-question test. The four players who get the most questions correct advance to the final table. (If a playoff is necessary, it's conducted in the form of a putting contest—partially because Max thinks it's the fairest way, but mainly because watching a bunch of blackjack pros with a piece of sporting equipment in their hands is a recipe for instant comedy.)

Any well-read gambling dilettante could conceivably ace Rubin's written test and find himself competing for the coveted Blackjack Cup. But the finals gracefully separate the hardcore professionals—those who spend most of their waking hours in casinos around the world betting the house limit—from those who merely make a good living at the game.

The final table is a practicum, a thorough test of the many requisite (and some not so requisite) skills a serious blackjack player must master to succeed in the real-world arena: counting down a deck in 20 seconds and identifying if a big, little, or neutral card has been removed; cutting exactly 21 cards out of a 52-card deck; playing expert strategy when all the 5s, 6s, 7s, and 8s

have been thrown out; tossing playing cards into a spit-
toon; memorizing a 13-card sequence; shuffling two pillars of chips with one hand; setting up a "cold" (pre-ar-
ranged) deck; figuring jackpot odds; and, in the interest
of "manliness," arm-wrestling the competition.

Since this is a convention of professional gamblers,
each contestant begins with $500 in casino chips and,
naturally, must wager on himself, varying his bet depending on his level of proficiency at each task. The player
with the most chips at the end of Rubin's blackjack Olym-
piad is the winner, and, until next year, the King of the
Ball.

Discretion prohibits me from accurately describing
the visage of this year's winner. Terry plies his trade
anonymously and would like to keep it that way. But
next time you're in a casino and see an altogether unre-
markable fellow with a mountain of chips before him,
minding his business and getting phenomenally "lucky,"
quietly mention Max Rubin's name. Mention the Blackjack Ball. And see if the nameless gambler offers you a
bottle of complimentary champagne.

THE TEST

Contestants at the Blackjack Ball must prove their
competency on a mostly multiple-choice test; top scorers advance to the next round. Here is a sample from the
actual 1999 test. If you score better than 50%, you may
have a future as a professional gambler.

1) Japanese consider it bad luck to stick your chop-
sticks straight up in your rice bowl, except at:
A. weddings
B. funerals
C. sumo wrestling matches
D. business meetings

2) True or False: In Thailand a good-luck amulet for strength and mastery of games is a crocodile penis.

3) Who is generally credited with making the statement, "Anything worth having is worth cheating for"?

   A. Dustin Marks
   B. Steve Forte
   C. Ken Uston
   D. W.C. Fields

4) Played perfectly, which game has the highest odds in favor of the house?

   A. roulette
   B. Caribbean Stud
   C. red dog
   D. Let It Ride

5) If you are triskaidekaphobic, what are you afraid of?

6) In Nevada, how much do you have to buy-in for before it is a "loggable transaction"?

   A. $1,000
   B. $2,500
   C. $10,000
   D. $10,001

7) True or False: Lucky numbers notwithstanding, in Las Vegas the average monthly video poker drop, per store, is higher at the 7-Eleven chain than any other convenience stores.

8) Which of these is the worst bet in a casino?
   A. craps "any seven"
   B. baccarat "tie bet"
   C. keno "eight spot"
   D. Let It Ride "side bet"

9) If you remove a five from a single deck, playing Las Vegas Strip rules, what advantage does it give to the player?
   A. .45%
   B. .55%
   C. .69%
   D. .88%

10) True or False: On Monday evening December 21, 1998, more people in the United States watched professional wrestling than "Monday Night Football."

ANSWERS:
   1: B; 2: True; 3: D; 4: B; 5: the number 13; 6: B; 7: False; 8: D; 9: C; 10: True.

The Poker Flower

Cyndy Violette plies her trade at a major Atlantic City hotel and casino. Given her line of work, it's the ideal place to do what she does best. She only comes in on weekends, sometimes toiling around the clock on Saturday night, when business is booming. Her prize customers—and there are many of them—are men. So many men she can barely remember their names or faces. An anonymous blur. They do, however, all have one thing in common: They have money. Lots of money. Money to throw around in search of entertainment, money to spend on a pretty lady. Many weekends she comes home from the casino with $10,000 or more than when she arrived. On a great weekend, sometimes much more.

You've probably deduced what Cyndy Violette does for a living. Most people, sexism firmly entrenched, can figure it out easily.

Most people, however, would be mistaken. Which is fine with Cyndy Violette. She doesn't mind that most people are misled by their sexism. Because it's this same sexism that often allows her to succeed in her profession far more richly than an equally talented man might.

Yes, Cyndy Violette is an attractive woman. She is also a high-stakes poker player. And that combination, as far as many of her less enlightened opponents are concerned, is not something that should be possible, not if they have anything to do with it.

Which is also fine with Cyndy Violette. Because she is delighted to teach them an extraordinarily expensive lesson.

Twenty-two years old. Unmarried. Pregnant. Dealing blackjack and poker at a downtown Las Vegas casino. She was broke, or as near to broke as a girl can be while still managing to find the necessary funds to play $1 and $2 poker.

Thanks to the little poker games, Cyndy Violette didn't stay broke for long.

She says of the early days, when a $50 windfall was cause for a riotous celebration, "I honestly had no idea what I was doing. I just always seemed to get lucky. I always seemed to win." This dumb luck—or undiscovered innate skill—gave Cyndy Violette the preposterous idea that she might make a living playing cards, that she might actually quit her punch-the-clock job and go into business for herself.

She knew such thoughts were crazy. After all, working as a dealer, she'd seen dozens of gamblers go broke trying to make the transition from amateur to professional. Even more discouraging, there were practically no women she could count as role models, members of the "wrong" gender doing everything right at the poker tables. Sure, there was Barbara Enright, a fierce competitor and the only woman to make it to the final table at the World Series of Poker world championship event; and yes, a handful of more or less anonymous ladies seemed to hold their own in the low- and middle-limit games. But these were anomalies. The truth was (and still is) this: Women generally don't play high-stakes poker, and when they do they don't last in the big games for very long. The competition is too tough, the pressure is too great, and the oppressive weight of sexism too heavy a burden to carry on petite shoulders.

But Cyndy Violette didn't know her place.

As her bankroll grew, so did the stakes at which she gambled. In less than six months, Violette was playing $15-$30 poker, where wins and losses in the thousands are not unusual. Shortly after her daughter Shannon was born, Cyndy Violette played in her first poker tournament, at Stateline, up at Lake Tahoe. It was supposed to be a fun little vacation. She finished in the top five.

"I knew then that I could probably make a career out of poker," she recalls. "And even if I couldn't, I was willing to try. I guess you could say I took a gamble."

After that first tournament triumph, Violette never went back to work. She moved permanently from the dealer's side of the table to the player's.

When Violette first began gambling in earnest, in the mid-'80s, the big seven-card stud games, her specialty, were $30-$60. Armed with a modest bankroll cobbled together from months of winning sessions at smaller stakes, Violette beat the game. (Beating a casino poker game does not mean winning each time you sit down; it means consistently winning more during your profitable sessions than you lose during your unprofitable ones.) Then $75-$150 games started popping up in Las Vegas. She beat those, too. These days, $150-$300 stakes are not uncommon in the biggest poker rooms. And it's not uncommon to see Cyndy Violette, with a stack of chips towering before her, beating those games, too.

You can't miss her at the table. She's the one who's about six inches shorter and at least 100 pounds lighter than the other gamblers betting, raising, and folding. And probably the only one who wears a brassiere.

Men have always been the primary obstacle between Cyndy Violette and success at high-stakes poker. Most of these fellows occupy seats around the green-felt ring. But one man in particular almost put her out of the game.

That would be Violette's ex-husband. Soon after cultivating her advanced poker skills, honing both her mathematical and psychological arsenal, young Cyndy fell in love. Her beaux was a gambler himself—someone, she thought, who understood a poker player's lifestyle. She married quickly and followed her groom to Washington state, where she assumed she would be a sometime homemaker, a sometime poker player, and an all-the-time wife. This, she soon learned, was not an assumption her husband shared.

Things started to go badly shortly after Cyndy had won a major tournament, reaping $62,000 for the victory. Her burgeoning gambling prowess combined with her good looks made her an enticing subject for any number of men's magazines, including *Playboy*, which proposed an article and photo layout. "They wanted to call it 'The Lady Shows Her Hole Cards,' or something silly like that," Violette laughs.

Per her husband's wishes, Cyndy Violette didn't gamble for two years. (Though she sat for an interview and a photo shoot, she didn't appear in *Playboy*, either.)

"I was forced into early retirement," Violette says. "At first it didn't bother me. I was happy being a mom and a wife. But eventually I got the itch."

She scratched it with a two-week vacation at the Bicycle Club in Los Angeles, which, at the time, spread a $75-$150 stud game, and to Caesars Palace, which, at the time, hosted a prestigious poker tournament called the Super Bowl of Poker. The first week of her vacation, Violette won $60,000 at the Bike. The second week, she won the Caesars tournament.

"I realized then that my marriage was pretty much over," she says.

After her divorce, Violette visited Atlantic City, which had recently legalized live poker. "I virtually lived at the Taj Mahal for two months," she says. "The games were so good. A lot of people had only played poker in home games before they came to the casino. They really didn't know what they were doing. And on the other hand, there were others who didn't care about the money. For them it was all irrelevant. The higher the limit, the less they cared."

To a professional poker player, the nascent Atlantic City poker scene was a dream come true. Cyndy Violette decided to move there permanently and set up shop.

She travels around the world, wherever a good game can be found. But she still calls Atlantic City—Absecon, a nearby suburb, actually—her home. And it is in Atlantic City that I meet her.

Cyndy Violette, 38, has made a living confounding expectations. So it probably shouldn't come as a surprise that when I join her at the Taj Mahal's steakhouse, she confesses she's a macrobiotic vegetarian. And a dedicated astrologist. And an herbal-massage junkie. "The casino lifestyle can be unhealthy," she warns. "But only if you let it. I work out regularly, eat well, and try to get plenty of sleep. Of course," she says, laughing, "when the game is good you've got to stay up."

Unlike many of her poker-playing brethren, Cyndy Violette only works on the weekends, when the big games are filled with visiting celebrities, household-name businessmen, and other assorted multi-millionaires willing to blow tens of thousands of dollars in search of a good time. "I usually play in the one-fifty-to-three-hundred or two-hundred-to-four-hundred games," Violette reports. "Sometimes it gets as high as four-hundred-to-eight-hundred. These games produce swings as high as thirty-thousand in a night. For me, that's plenty."

The rest of Violette's week, she says, is devoted to her racehorses (one of which is named Poker Chip), working on her house (which has both a lagoon pool and a duck pond), spending time with her now teenaged daughter, and attending lectures and workshops on health and wellness. "Someday I'd like to open my own health-food cafe," she says.

The capital she's amassed recently will go far toward those goals. In recent months, at the United States Poker Championships, Violette won the seven-card-stud event, conquering 207 opponents. She also "cashed" in three other events, making the final table (the remaining eight or nine players) each time.

"It was a good tournament," she says, modestly.

Good, indeed, considering that the competition in tournaments like the U.S. Poker Championships and the World Series of Poker, where Violette is also a familiar face, consists of the best card players in the world—almost all of them men.

"Sometimes it's an advantage to be a woman poker player," Violette confides. "Seeing a woman across the table seems to trigger something in a lot of male egos. They either want to beat you hard or take it easy on you. Either they don't give you any credit for your ability or they give you way too much credit. Women get much more action than men; a lot more hands get paid off." Violette smiles, amused that such foolishness still works to her benefit. "Guys that normally wouldn't play in a big poker game will jump right in. They figure the game is soft!"

Is it just her gender that puts men on tilt, or is it, more precisely, her appearance? "Being attractive is a productive distraction, I guess," Violette admits. "But I think it would work the same for a good-looking man."

At her recent U.S. Poker Championship victories, Violette didn't suffer any of the indignities she has sometimes endured at poker tables in the past: no verbal barbs; no overt rudeness; no mean-spirited pot-shots. She has earned the competition's respect over the years and, particularly in Atlantic City, she is something of a card-playing celebrity. "Winning in front of my friends and family was nice," she says. "But I like winning anywhere."

Besides her daughter, one of Violette's biggest fans is the owner of the casino where she most regularly works: Donald Trump. Violette, Trump says, is one of his favorite Taj Mahal regulars —for obvious reasons. "I think it's tremendous that she's such a fine player," he tells me. "And the fact that she's a woman makes it even more tremendous."

While Trump is no poker player himself, he professes a deep respect for the skills a world-class player like Violette possesses. "I think people like Cyndy who are used to making big decisions under pressure would do very well in the business world." The casino magnate, in fact, has solicited her advice on several Taj poker-room-related issues and, according to Violette, has acted on her suggestions.

"Donald says hello whenever he's in town," Violette reports. "I'd say we're friendly."

Atlantic City is a living annuity for players like Cyndy Violette. The high-limit players are generally greener than other parts of America; big games get off virtually every weekend; and the Trump Taj Mahal treats its customers well, providing table-side masseuses and cooked-to-order meals. Still, Violette admits she's mulling a move to Las Vegas, where she's a regular visitor.

"And even if I don't move there permanently, you can bet I'll be at the World Series of Poker every spring," she promises. "I've got to play in the women's world-championship event. I've done a lot in poker and had a lot of success. But," she says, shrugging, "I've never won a ladies tournament."

High Roller

10

With apologies to the United States Constitution, the Bill of Rights, and every other good and noble document our blessed country has produced in the pursuit of fairness and decency, all men are *not* created equal.

At least not in Las Vegas.

Here in the Land of Anything's Possible, a caste system as rigid and unforgiving as India's separates the Worthy Few from the Unwashed Mob—and it's got nothing to do with anything as spurious as patrician bloodlines or precinct of birth. It's all about money. Old, new, ill-begotten, it doesn't matter. You got it? Your limo is waiting! You don't? Right this way to the back of the taxi line, pal.

Picture, if you will, an enormous pyramid—like Luxor, before they put that hideous ziggurat beside it. At the wide base is the foundation upon which the gambling economy is based: the low-rollers. They seek out the $9.95 steak-and-lobster specials, nickel slots, and buy-the-glass-get-free-refills drink deals. They bring a pre-determined amount of gambling money that they expect to lose and schedule their play around how long it lasts. If they see a headliner or dine at one of the gourmet restaurants, they generally pay full retail for the privilege.

Higher up the pyramid, where it starts to get a bit narrower, are the mid rollers, the $50-and-up bettors who stay in the tonier joints, get a discount (sometimes a 100% discount) on their room rate, and can often talk their way into free tickets to the house production show and a nice dinner in a room other than the buffet.

Then, near the pointy top, where angels fear to tread, are the vaunted high rollers.

Everyone claims to know a high roller or two; everyone has an aunt who gets invitations to no-entry-fee slot tournaments, or a colleague at work who gets all his rooms for free, or a buddy in the entertainment business who occasionally bets with black chips and gets VIP passes to Studio 54 and Club Rio.

The true high roller, however, is the gambler who has earned "RFB" (complimentary room, food, and beverage) status at a top Strip hotel, a gambler who signs-and-goes and never sees the charge show up on his bill. A gambler who enjoys the best of everything in Las Vegas, courtesy of the casinos.

Where the Luxor's billion-watt light shines out toward the Mojave sky would be the highest-of-the-highs, known as "whales," guys who are capable of betting $200,000 a hand. There are only about 50 of them in the world, and they don't want to talk with an ink-stained wretch like me.

Though they're the ones best equipped to pay for $300 bottles of wine, $500 fight tickets, and $1,200-a-night accommodations, high rollers typically pay exactly zero for the tastiest fruits Las Vegas has to offer. You could use any number of apposite clichés to explain this phenomenon—"the rich get richer"; "it's good to be king"; "life ain't fair"—but there's a simpler way to look at the life

of a Vegas high roller: "You get what you pay for."
Just ask Buddy.

All-you-can-gorge buffets do not interest him. Two-for-one tickets to the afternoon Elvis show do not interest him. Discounted weekend room rates of $49 per night do not interest him. Yet Buddy MacDonald [some names and identifying details have been changed] will tell anyone who will listen that Las Vegas is "the greatest entertainment value in the world." His thinking goes something like this: Where else can an ignorant degenerate fool like me be treated like an esteemed head of state, a member of visiting royalty, a distinguished man of letters and science? A celebrity?

Vegas has mastered the art of making a regular Joe feel as though he's someone he isn't. If only for a weekend, the real-estate agent from Milwaukee can be James Bond; the divorced mother of two from Seattle can be Grace Kelly; Buddy MacDonald, wildly successful owner of a decidedly un-sexy Orange County, California, electrical-contracting business, can be the sexiest dude on the Strip, flush with a penthouse suite, gourmet meals, knee-weakening escorts, and the kind of fawning "yes, sir!" attention typically reserved for members of the better country clubs.

"They make me feel like I'm appreciated," Buddy confirms.

The dirty little secret, though, is that the marketing executives and hosts and maitre d's who shower Buddy with love are not much different than the expensive prostitutes he hires during his weekend bacchanalia: What they "appreciate" is Buddy's money—particularly his uncanny ability to lose it at the gambling tables. High rollers—a term originally applied to big-betting dice players—are to Las Vegas what Vermeer paintings are to museum curators: rare highly prized acquisitions that add luster (and profits) to the endowment. Buddy MacDonald is *wanted*. And any Las Vegas casino lucky enough to have him as a customer is eager to show Buddy just how well-loved he truly is.

The affection begins with his arrival at McCarran Airport, where a uniformed driver meets Buddy at the baggage claim. (Buddy is a very big bettor—but not quite big enough to warrant a chartered jet; instead, the casino asks that Buddy purchase a first-class ticket on the airline of his choice and let them reimburse him for travel expenses at the end of his stay.) Rather than departing through the street-level doors that most Vegas visitors use, Buddy and his chauffeur go down one level to an area known as "Ground Zero," where a fleet of limousines awaits, like so many golden chariots ready to whisk Roman generals off to their next conquest. Buddy's car this spring evening has a television and a bar and a stereo, all of which might come in handy if the trip to the hotel were more than five minutes.

Tonight, Buddy is headed for Bellagio, his current "home away from home" in Las Vegas. He has previously been a guest of MGM Grand, Caesars Palace, and the Venetian. Indeed, whenever a new property opens in Las Vegas, Buddy gets a call inviting him to be part of the festivities. "I don't know how they get my number," he says, chuckling. "I guess I have a reputation." In the past, Buddy admits to having played one casino off the other, seeing who would "take the best care of me, who wanted my business the most." Soon, he discovered, *every* place would take extraordinarily good care of him, including granting him a small rebate on his gambling losses. "I'm happy at Bellagio," he says. "They take care of everything. It has great restaurants, great rooms—and great golf."

One of the perquisites that MGM Mirage properties

can offer its customers is a round at Shadow Creek golf club, the super-exclusive North Las Vegas fantasyland created for the pleasure and privacy of Steve Wynn's friends and honored guests. Up until a few years ago the only way to enjoy a round at this vaunted playground was by invitation—and that came only if you were a friend of the corporation or an RFB player at one of its casinos. Now, any old hacker with a credit card can play the course, assuming he's willing to pay the $1,000 green fee. (Hey, it includes a room for one night and limo transportation to and from the links.) Buddy, like every other RFB guest at MGM Mirage properties, is entitled to visit Shadow Creek whenever he likes without any charge, and before the weekend is over he will avail himself of the Creek's pristine sod.

Upon arrival at Bellagio, Buddy skips the usual check-in procedures most Vegas visitors must endure. A smartly dressed (and absurdly attractive) young woman from the VIP Services office greets Buddy at the door, holding a small packet containing his room keys and a "welcome-back" note from the casino manager. (Buddy's "details" are already on file, as is his excellent credit history. Indeed, the bulk of the funds with which he will gamble has already been wired to the cage directly from one of Buddy's bank accounts, and if he needs more he'll just sign readily proffered markers.) His suite this weekend—"my usual place" he calls it—is a one-bedroom, two-bathroom, six-telephone spread, as large as many single-family homes with significantly more furniture. After glimpsing Buddy's weekend digs, the old myth that "they build Vegas hotel room small so you won't want to stay in them" has never seemed more ridiculous: You could host a party for 100 fabulous friends here, if only you knew that many people who would appreciate the view of Bellagio's faux Lake Como and the dancing waters below.

Instead of ordering complimentary room service and

soaking in the Jacuzzi, Buddy is eager to visit the gambling tables. Without unpacking his suitcase—"they got a butler who will do it for you," he reports—Buddy grabs an apple from the enormous fruit basket the hotel has waiting for him on his suite's dining room table and dashes for the private elevator.

As on most Friday evenings, the casino is crowded, frenetic with the hum of clattering chips and buzzing slot machines and the staccato yelps of inspired gamblers. But where Buddy plays, the high-limit baccarat salon, there's an air of refinement and sophistication. The croupiers wear tuxedos; floor supervisors welcome players deferentially and speak in hushed tones; the lighting is indirect and soothing. You could almost imagine you were in some ethereal corner of Europe, except for the presence of two well-capitalized Texans chatting loudly about the NCAA basketball tournament.

Buddy signs a marker for $100,000 in chips. "Just to get my feet wet," he jokes nervously. He's a millionaire many times over; were he to lose every one of the colorful discs before him—which he has done often in his gambling "career"—it wouldn't change his lifestyle in the slightest. (In fact, he'd just sign for more and try to recoup his losses.) But it's enough money to "get my heart beating, get the adrenaline flowing." And, perhaps equally important, enough to afford him "the treatment." Within twenty minutes of settling into a plush high-backed chair at the baccarat table, Buddy's host strides into the room, all smiles and twinkling eyes, toting a day-timer as thick as a prime steak. "Mr. MacDonald," the host says, extending a hand, "just wanted to say hello, and, you know, make sure everything was all right. The room? It's all—everything's fine, right?"

"Yeah, very nice," Buddy says, barely looking up from the table to shake his host's hand.

"And let's see," the host thumbs through his day-timer, "I've got you down here for a late dinner at Picasso tonight. Table for two, right?"

"Yeah, great," Buddy says. "I've been hearing some good things about that place."

"Oh sure. Great reviews. Lots of awards," the host chirps. And he can't help adding, "Very tough table these days."

For a customer like Buddy, however, nothing is too tough. If he wants something he gets it—which is a delightful difference from the real world, where instant gratification isn't necessarily the way things work, no matter how wealthy you are. The host departs, saying, "I don't want to disturb you any longer"—code for "The longer I chat with you the less you gamble." This leaves Buddy to the crucial business of trying to pick which hand will have a point total closest to 9. Buddy says, "You gotta love it, huh?"

Yes, you do. Just as the casino has "gotta love" a customer like Mr. MacDonald.

He wagers between $1,000 and $10,000 a hand, including frequent plunges on the "tie" proposition, a sucker bet that gives the house a hefty 14.4% advantage. (The "player" and "bank" bets at baccarat give the house closer to a 1% edge.) There seems to be no rationale to explain why Buddy sometimes bets a little and sometimes a lot. Like other baccarat players, he studies a chart in which he tracks the results of past hands, staring at it intently as he bites his lower lip, somehow convincing himself he can divine a pattern in the random succession of wins and losses. Anyone with a high-school-math-student's understanding of rudimentary probabilities should be able to figure out that no amount of chart analysis can turn a negative expectation game like baccarat into a winning proposition, that the past results have no bearing on future results. But Buddy—and every other high roller in the baccarat pit—seems willfully ignorant of this basic truth. Or willfully unwilling to care. Sometimes he wins; sometimes he loses. But in the long run the house gets the money.

And this is why Buddy MacDonald is entitled to the treatment he enjoys. According to Max Rubin, author of *Comp City*, an expose of the Las Vegas comp system, a player like Buddy, who averages about $4,000 a hand at baccarat, is "worth" more than $50,000 in expected losses over a typical weekend. Since the casinos are usually willing to return around 30% of his losses in the form of complimentaries, Buddy, according to Rubin, has "earned himself quite a few fun tickets at the carnival."

Literally. There's a big fight card over at MGM Grand. When Buddy decides he wants to go, six hours before the bouts begin, he's furnished with ringside center seats, directly behind Goldie Hawn, Kevin Costner, and the fight's promoter Bob Arum, not to mention the best customers of every other casino in town. Most of the high rollers in attendance—including Buddy—have in tow what look to be terribly expensive companions who, contrary to a popular misconception, are *not* paid for by the casinos. (The casinos will gladly, shall we say, "make introductions" for their best customers, but in the modern, publicly traded, corporate Vegas, the fees for services rendered are strictly the client's responsibility.) Buddy's "date" is a dead-ringer for Sarah Jessica Parker, with slightly larger breasts and, based on the cocktail-napkin-of-a-skirt she wears, an even shapelier derrière. According to the high roller from Orange County, she is worth "every penny" of the $2,000 he pays her for the pleasure of an evening's company.

It's all worth it. He may lose a little. He may win a little. He might win a lot. He might very well lose even more. But no matter what he does or where he goes when he's in Las Vegas, it always feels good.

Every time he sips the first-growth Bordeaux at

Picasso and occupies the fifth-row-center seats at Cirque du Soleil's *O* and fills a bubble bath in his suite out of the bottles of Dom Perignon shipped to his room like so many fresh flowers, it's all courtesy of the casino. Every time he orders a floorman to scrounge up a good Cuban cigar or has a cocktail waitress bring him another glass of the $100-a-shot single-malt whisky or requests ever so ingenuously if his host might secure a last-minute reservation for him and Sarah Jessica to Le Cirque—it all feels good. For 48 hours Buddy MacDonald isn't a successful electrical contractor with a wife and three children and two dogs and a gerbil. He's a Las Vegas high roller, and there's nowhere else he'd rather be.

Holy Macau!

Hydrofoils from Hong Kong depart for the island of Macau every day of the year, every hour of the day, every fifteen minutes. The ride across the South China Sea is remarkably smooth and pleasantly scenic. But the hundreds of passengers who take this train-on-the-water aren't interested in the craggy shoreline or the lumbering fishing boats the hydrofoil leaves in its wake. Like children in the backseat of the family station wagon, they just want to get there.

Because Macau, a Portuguese protectorate for more than 400 years until it was handed back to China in 1999, has something you can't find in Hong Kong: casinos.

These are not genteel European parlors or spacious American-style ballrooms, outfitted with plush carpets and ersatz chandeliers. They're gambling factories. A few of the island's eight casinos are the size of a decent Wal-Mart—and most have about as many "shoppers." Even on an otherwise tranquil Sunday afternoon, the casinos of Macau are easily the most crowded gambling joints you've ever seen, with bettors three and four deep at every table, elbowing their countrymen aside to get some money on the sacred green felt. An uninitiated visitor from, say, Las Vegas might presume the casinos had some sort of generous promotion in force—blackjack pays 2-1, perhaps—or that they had momentarily lost their finely calibrated sense of larceny and were simply giving away money. But closer inspection reveals the action at the tables is merely business as usual. The thousands of patrons clamoring to get their bets down just really like to gamble.

That is to say they *really* like to gamble. I mean, they are stone-cold-out-of-their-minds crazy about gambling.

The casinos of Macau are easily the most animated wagering palaces you've ever seen. On hands of chemin de fer (known as "baccarat" along Las Vegas Boulevard), opposing sides shout friendly curses at each other in Cantonese, trying vainly to change the spots on a fateful card. Applause and groaning accompany the outcome of each hand—and it's not polite routine-par-on-the-PGA-Tour applause, or mock I-didn't-really-need-that-money groaning, either. This is the real stuff. The actors in Macau's quotidian drama emote so convincingly because they care so profoundly about every hand. Which is understandable, since most bets here seem to represent a sizable portion of the protagonists' life savings.

The minimum wager at most tables is between $15 and $25. But nobody bets the minimum. Even young men, very young men, in their late teens maybe, who proudly wear "American Original Playboy Spirit" windbreakers and have cultivated something resembling a moustache above their tender lips—even these lads wager sums that would make the typical Vegas high roller feel like a candidate for the all-you-can-eat buffet line. The prevailing thinking among the gamblers here seems to be, "Small is bad; big is good." The nearer your wager to the house maximum (US$100,000 in the VIP rooms), the nearer, it seems, to nirvana. Even the chips, laminated plastic discs the size of your kitchen sink drain, seem to suggest that bigger is indeed better.

This compulsion to plunge it all away on the bounce of a ball or the turn of a domino, according to several residents of Hong Kong, can be explained as an obscure symptom of the city's absurd real-estate market. One young professional, a bond trader who pays more than $100,000 a year in rent for his high-rise apartment, says, "Even if you have a decent job, you can't afford to ever buy a decent apartment. So you gamble. In Hong Kong you have to gamble if you want to keep up."

Then there's the no-nonsense point of view. "We Chinese, we just love to gamble," says Tony Liu, Vice President of Oriental Marketing at the Trump Taj Mahal, in Atlantic City. "Win or lose, we don't care. We just love to play. And as long as we have some money in front of us, we won't stop."

Though most ethnic generalizations are about as trustworthy as loaded dice, anyone in the gaming business will tell you there are no more "dedicated" players than the Chinese. Indeed, most Chinese gamblers will tell you the same thing. "We're born to gamble," says Danny, a "dedicated" gambler who works in management at a Hong Kong hotel. "Chinese don't fool around. We come to win, to make a big score. It's in our blood."

According to Larry Clark, the Taj Mahal's Executive Vice President of Casino Operations, whose Dragon Room caters to high-rolling Asians, casinos across America would love to capture even a small slice of the Oriental market. Outside of California, where special Asian-games sections draw concert-size crowds, the Taj's Dragon Room is among the largest Asian gambling arenas outside of Asia. "I was inspired by the Asian games I'd seen in Macau, and I wanted to recreate the atmosphere of excitement and mystique," Clark says.

In one respect he's been hugely successful. The

Dragon Room, like its antecedents in Macau, is always packed. On a typical weekend night or early morning, every seat at every table is occupied, with an eager crowd waiting for space to become available. Not surprisingly, Tony Liu, the marketer, says he has more than 20,000 names in his database of invited guests.

Fifteen times a year, the Taj puts on Asian-themed shows in its convention-center showroom, featuring the Madonnas and Tony Bennetts of China, Vietnam, and the Philippines. These extravaganzas, which consistently attract audiences of 4,000, usually don't begin until 2 a.m., when most Atlantic City revelers are contemplating the charms of a final cognac and a down pillow. Tony Liu explains, "Many of our customers close their shops and restaurants around ten or eleven. We have to give them time to drive here."

This preference for late-night revelries is just one of the stylistic differences between Occidental and Oriental bettors. Most Western gamblers like the casino's complimentary booze; Asian gamblers prefer coffee. Most Westerners are mildly health conscious; players in the casinos of Macau (and the casinos that would imitate them) smoke like overheated engines. Most Westerners play for three or four hours at a stretch; Hong Kongers in Macau bet for up to 48 hours straight—or until they've gone bust. Westerners generally like slots and craps and blackjack; the Chinese players love an inscrutable domino game called Pai Gow. If a Westerner has $20,000 to his name, he might be willing to play with $5,000 of it (and that's if he's a wild man); if a Chinese guy has $20,000 to his name, he'll bet at least that much, and more if he's got a good line of credit.

"There's no bigger gamblers than the Chinese," Larry Clark says. "Any culture with a Judeo-Christian background, gambling has a stigma. With the Chinese it's accepted. It's a way of life."

Nothing illustrates Clark's assertion better than a visit to the Happy Valley racetrack, wedged surreally beneath a field of skyscrapers in the heart of Hong Kong. A typical Wednesday night of horse racing draws close to 50,000 screaming patrons; weekend programs at the Sha Tin horse-racing complex, in a nearby suburb, draw as many as 90,000 spectators. And they're not just watching the ponies run around in circles. In 1997, the Hong Kong Jockey Club, which manages the racetracks, handled more than HK$93 billion in wagers.

That's about US$12 billion.

According to Henry Chan, the Jockey Club's Director of Betting, "Horse racing is a way of life for us. It's entertainment and it's sport. But even more it's like an art. Chinese people love to study the forms, to handicap the races. It's really our national sport."

As the only legalized form of gambling in Hong Kong beside a national lottery, the racetracks are highly regulated—and, of course, highly profitable. (Hong Kong's one-day betting record is currently US$326,810,000.) Each year the Jockey Club donates HK$1-$2 billion to the community. Proceeds from horse racing helped build the Hong Kong University of Science and Technology, the Castle Peak Hospital and the Hong Kong Football Stadium. In fact, the Hong Kong Jockey Club is among the top-ten charitable foundations in the world.

This becomes possible when, in a country with a total population of 6 million, 750,000 people have telephone betting accounts and a million people bet each race day at one of 125 off-course outlets.

The Chinese cultural stereotype—highly superstitious, fascinated by the concept of luck—may have some truth to it, Chan concedes. "But horses are a game of skill. And besides," Chan adds, "Chinese don't see betting on horses as 'gambling.' It's *playing*. We work hard and we play hard. Here in Hong Kong we have small homes and little leisure time. A day at the races is a most civilized relief from our hectic lives."

Given this kind of nationwide equine fervor, casino gambling is hardly necessary, Chan says. "The government doesn't want to encourage additional gambling in Hong Kong. We wish Macau was even farther away," he says, laughing.

Chan's dream notwithstanding, millions of other residents of this frenetic city find their escape across the water, far from the exactas and quinellas of Happy Valley. They go to Macau, where an instant fortune is only a turn of a card away.

Many of the games in the casinos here are difficult for Western eyes to decipher. Some, like Pai Gow, are played with dominoes, which the locals slap, fondle, and when they really need a winner, caress like small birds, reading the dots with their fingers instead of their eyes. Others, like Dai-Siu, employ dice, and players bet if the total of three die will be "big" or "small." The odds, you can be sure, are skewed worse than the prop bets on a crap table, not that anyone in Macau seems to mind terribly.

The most peculiar of these casino games is called Fan Tan, an ancient Chinese diversion made modern by the presence of croupiers, pit bosses, and hordes of eager gamblers. The dealer covers a large pile of porcelain buttons with a silver cup, pushes the shrouded pile toward the center of the table, and removes the cover, like a waiter in a classical French restaurant. He then divides the pile of buttons into groups of four. Players bet on whether, after the division, there will be 0, 1, 2, or 3 remaining buttons.

Much frivolity is enjoyed by all, especially the studious types, who keep dense detailed charts of the results, which, they suppose, help divine a pattern in the sublime randomness of the button pile.

Whereas most casinos in America are wall-to-wall slot machines, few of what the Chinese call "hungry tigers" line the walls of Macau's casinos. They seem like so many forlorn afterthoughts, homely girls waiting to be asked for a dance. The handful of video poker machines are even lonelier, and for good reason. Most gamblers here have no concept of basic strategy, and even if they did it would do them no good. The pay tables are laughable—6 coins for a full house, 5 for a flush—and most machines have a "war" feature that encourages players to double their winnings by challenging the machine to a game of "high card wins." This being Macau, most players gladly do battle until they blithely convert their profits into nothing.

Blackjack games are rare. On a recent visit, the Casino Jai Alai, a warehouse-size emporium near the ferry terminal, had one blackjack table. The Mandarin Oriental had two.

The rules are surprisingly good—dealer stands on soft 17; surrender available against a dealer 10—but card-counting is ineffectual, since the dealer burns a card on every hand and three of the eight decks in play get cut off, drastically reducing penetration. Not that professional card counters would want to ply their trade here, anyway. The casinos of Macau, operated under a government franchise by the Sociedade de Turismo e Diversoes de Macau, are controlled by a man named Stanley Ho. It is widely rumored in both Hong Kong and the States that Mr. Ho has intimate relationships with plenty of unsavory characters. "The last place you would want to try anything clever is Macau," one professional blackjack player, based in Nevada, says. "Ho is richer than God, and almost as powerful."

White-skinned gamblers, do, in fact, stand out from the crowd, if only because of sheer novelty. Most of the Chinese gamblers, Scotch-taping their chips into tidy stacks before firing off $20,000 bets on a hand of baccarat, are too busy tempting fate (and bad odds) to pay attention to a stray "ghost." At Casino Lisboa, a four-story gambling emporium with higher limits the farther up you ride the escalator, the only denizens of the place that seem interested in Western visitors are dozens of hookers, who have mastered the rudiments of roulette, as well as the English phrases "happy time" and "go to my room."

The pungently charged atmosphere in Macau is redolent of the old Vegas: fast money, fast women, reality blurred by the intoxicating clatter of chips and dice and dominoes. But lest a daydreaming visitor imagine he's been magically transported to Nevada back when gangsters called the shots and hedonism flowed as freely as wine at a bacchanal, signs posted on the casino's walls announce in no uncertain terms that this isn't the Fabulous Flamingo circa 1946, but a wild gambling-drunk island off the coast of China. In three languages they say, "Please do not spit on the floor."

Who Really Wants To Be A Millionaire?

12

I don't know what pains me more: Walking through a Las Vegas casino on a Friday night, seeing hundreds (thousands?) of piteous losers attached to slot machines like so many intensive-care patients on a morphine drip; or watching ABC on Sundays, Tuesdays, and Thursdays, seeing dozens (hundreds?) of otherwise very smart people make one costly gambling mistake after another.

The pop-culture sensation known as "Who Wants to Be a Millionaire" is missing a question mark in its title. The vast majority of contestants who appear on the show seem to be missing the boat.

What I see night after night is the equivalent of someone taking two large handfuls of $100 bills and throwing them into the middle of the Strip. (Naïve slot players do the same thing, but their willingness to leave money laying in the street is expressed in far less dramatic fashion. They just piss it away a nickel or a dime or a quarter at a time. The contestants on "Millionaire" blow their money grandly, operatically, epically. And on national television.

Yes, blow their money.

I'm not talking about someone who valiantly works his way up the ladder of questions to the $250,000 level and then answers incorrectly. I'm talking about those silly players—and there are surprisingly plenty of them—who don't answer at all, who "take the money and run" when the right thing to do is venture a guess.

What these contestants don't realize is that from an expected-value perspective, far from "taking the money," they're actually dashing off prematurely, leaving a good portion of what's rightfully theirs behind in host Regis Philbin's manicured fingers.

This happens, I assert, because the very smart people who make it through the long-odds screening process and into the "hot seat" know infinitely more about otherwise useless trivia questions than about a few basic gambling concepts. I would have thought that anyone bright enough to pass the phone test, win the phone play-off with other qualified entrants, and beat nine other smarty-pants types to make it into the money-chair would have taken a moment or two before their trip to New York City to analyze how to best use their lifelines. And how to make educated guesses. And, most importantly, when to guess and when to walk.

Strangely, with an alarming regularity that reminds me of slot players, the knowledgeable contestants on "Millionaire" consistently prove that their heads have been too inextricably buried in almanacs and oceanic maps to have considered the very real possibility that they might get to a certain level in the game and not know the correct answer. Or at least not be utterly sure of it. Based on observing almost every episode of the show, exactly three contestants have demonstrated that they know the right thing to do when they're less than 100% positive that they know the winning answer.

I say "the right thing to do" instead of "best thing" or

"safest thing" or "most telegenic thing" because "Millionaire" has an immutably correct "basic strategy" that yields for the player the highest expectation against the game. Just as there is one mathematically best play for every combination of player total and dealer upcard in blackjack, there is one best decision for every situation on "Millionaire." Hunches, suppositions, and fanciful theories proposed by your Uncle Jed (the one the casinos treat like visiting royalty) do not obviate "Millionaire's" blunt mathematics. If you make the right play, you optimize your "return on investment"; if you don't, you cost yourself money.

To quickly review: Players on the show answer multiple-choice questions with prize values that roughly double at each succeeding step. Miss a question and you're reduced to one of two plateau levels: $1,000, which is locked in after answering five questions correctly; or $32,000 which is locked in after answering 10 questions correctly. Each contestant gets three "lifelines," a trio of diverse and extremely helpful methods of getting an answer a player does not otherwise know. (On "Who Wants to Be a Millionaire," being really good at trivia helps, too. But as numerous players have proven, even without much more than average skill, judicious use of lifelines can earn an otherwise dull contestant a spectacular payday.)

From a gambling-odds perspective, the "50/50" lifeline, which removes two wrong answers, is the most reliable of the trio; the "phone-a-friend" lifeline, which allows the contestant to call a smart colleague (who, if he's really smart, should be sitting in front of a high-speed computer surrounded by a roomful of smart cohorts), is probably the next most powerful tool; and the "ask-the-audience" lifeline, which allows the contestant to poll 200 strangers, is the least powerful.

Some of the small (but costly) mistakes contestants

make involve the use of these aids. For example, although a plurality of the audience is right about 80% of the time, they're typically polled only on easy questions. The audience is a good barometer for the low-level pop-culture-type questions, but you wouldn't want their help on, say, a Shakespeare question. Nonetheless, anyone with a rudimentary grasp of probability should realize that when a random group of people who ostensibly have no special knowledge of a subject return their votes, the percentages for each answer should be 25%. Now, if one of the answers gets more than 50% of the vote and the other three hover around 17%, this is a strong indicator that they have a (collective) handle on the subject. In other words, the audience might be mistaken, but they probably aren't. Thus, this lifeline has served its purpose—highlighting what is likely to be the right answer. (Conversely, if two choices get nearly 50% of the vote or three get 33%, then the results should be dismissed.) Despite being furnished with such strong mathematical evidence, I see countless contestants ignore the audience vote because, the contestants often feebly explain, they were "hoping for a more convincing majority."

Similar gaffes include using the phone-a-friend to confirm a choice the contestant is already "pretty sure" (80% certain) about, thereby diluting the full value of the lifeline; using the phone-a-friend after narrowing the choices to 50/50, thereby diluting the full value of two lifelines; burning *any* lifeline on the "free" $64,000 question when it's more than 50% probable that you know the answer; and wasting the audience lifeline on subject matters other than popular culture or any other subject that would be familiar to a population that is more likely to subscribe to *People* magazine than *Atlantic Monthly*.

These are all small errors, the equivalent of not hitting a 16 versus a dealer's 10-up in blackjack. Other mistakes on "Millionaire" are much worse.

The most egregiously wrong thing to do on this show is to not take full advantage of the guaranteed money plateau at $32,000. Even if you're out of lifelines, everyone—even Regis—knows that when faced with the $64,000 question, you should take a guess. It's a $32,000 free-roll. Get it right and you've won $32,000 more than you previously had. Get it wrong and you still leave with $32,000. You're risking $0 to win $32,000.

It's at the next level, the $125,000 question, where I see the most money being squandered by the show's contestants. Granted, people get nervous when the very real prospect of winning a six-figure prize looms before them, but here are the facts.

By rule, if a contestant has won $64,000, the smallest amount he can leave with is $32,000. Thus, a wrong answer at the $125,000 level costs the player only $32,000. If, on the other hand, he gets the question right, he wins an additional $61,000—nearly twice as much as he stands to lose. In odds terms, you're getting 2-1 on your money. (Technically, it's not *exactly* 2-1; that would require the 12th question to be worth $128,000, which, I suppose, doesn't seem quite as elegant to the producers as $125,000. But it's pretty close.) To break even on this proposition, a player would have to answer the question correctly one out of three times. If he's able to answer the question correctly one out of two times—being right as often as he is wrong—he's getting an enormous "overlay," as gamblers like to say.

"Millionaire," you may recall, poses questions in a multiple-choice format, providing contestants with three incorrect choices and the correct one. Even with no knowledge whatsoever of a subject, a contestant who guesses will do so correctly one out of four times. (Remember, at the $125,000 level, players need only answer correctly one out of three times to break even.) If, however, he's able to eliminate one or more incorrect choices, he's drastically improved his chances. Indeed, with the help of the 50/50 lifeline, which eliminates two wrong answers, leaving one wrong answer and the correct one on the board, the player has an even-money (1-1) shot to pick the winner.

In this case, the correct play is clearly to guess. Flip a coin. Play eeny-meeny-miney-moe. Whatever. It doesn't matter how the choice is made—just so long as a choice *is* made. Being paid 2-1 on an even-money shot is about the best proposition you'll find in the gambling universe.

Looking at the $125,000 question from a purely mathematical perspective, when the contestant has narrowed the choices to 50/50, a guess is clearly warranted. But what of the emotional and practical perspectives?

Many trivia mavens are hesitant—if not downright ashamed—to admit they don't know an answer, and even more loath to answer wrongly. If you're brave enough to exhibit your vast store of knowledge on national television, you probably have a positive opinion of your mental powers and would hate to do anything that appears to diminish your trivia omniscience. But as most successful poker players, blackjack professionals, backgammon champions, golf hustlers—anyone who gambles for a living—will testify, there's little room for such emotion in an arena where rationale and logic carry the day. In other words, you probably have no business attempting to win the $1 million top prize on "Who Wants to Be a Millionaire" if you cannot divorce your heart from your head. Because your heart invariably won't let your head win.

Practically speaking, a lot of very smart people invoke a concept called "utility theory" to justify less than optimal decision-making. Utility theory basically says that if the money you stand to lose could be better used in your real life than in a highly positive gambling proposition (where, despite a big advantage, you could very well lose your stake), then it's better not to gamble at all. My position is this: Either you believe in the concept of expected value or you don't; it doesn't apply only when you're comfortable. Utility-theory apologists say, "The thirty-two thousand I could lose would pay for my kid's college education. I really shouldn't be gambling with it!" Expected value advocates say, "The hundred thousand or so you're refusing to accept could pay for that education and a lot more!"

Yes, $100,000 or more.

By not taking a shot at the $125,000 question, a player is not merely costing himself $14,500 (the difference between the expected value of guessing with a 50/50 chance, and simply walking with $64,000). He's costing himself tens of thousands in future *equity*, which is a term gamblers use to describe financial potential.

Here's why. A player who correctly answers the $125,000 question gets to look at the $250,000 question. Even without any remaining lifelines, he has a very real chance of knowing the answer, particularly if he's knowledgeable enough to have gotten this far already. The $250,000 may be about a subject dear to him or a piece of information he recently saw in a newspaper article or something he remembers from high-school biology class. Or he may be able to deduce the correct answer by throwing out the ones he knows to be incorrect. In that case he gets a free look at the $500,000 question. In fact, the equity consideration is so strong, it's worth guessing at the $125,000 question if you can only narrow it down to three answers, where the expected value of a guess is just $63,000 (a grand less than the locked-in $64,000).

Basic strategy also dictates that a player guess at the remaining levels, assuming the field can be narrowed to two choices. Thanks to the guaranteed $32,000, he's getting a reasonable overlay—and, again, the equity is huge. While there's an argument to be made that equity also makes it proper to guess in one-out-of-three situations further down the line, a precipitous drop in expected value (at levels above $125,000) likely justifies stopping when a player is less than 50% sure.

Setting aside questions of a player's intelligence or knowledge or deductive powers, these informed (and narrowed-down) guesses represent great gambling propositions. It's similar to certain arbitrage opportunities that sometimes occur in sports betting. For example, with no handicapping knowledge whatsoever, without even an understanding of the rules of the game, someone who is offered the opportunity to lay 2.5 points on the favorite and take 3.5 points on the underdog in NFL football will show a tidy profit at season's end, since, historically, the final result lands on 3 in the NFL games in which the line is 3 far more often than the one-out-of-20 times necessary to break even. Similarly, even if you know absolutely nothing about NBA basketball, if you couldn't tell the difference between a zone defense and an end zone, getting 3 points and laying 2 on the same game will turn a slim profit (even after the bookie's take).

In "Millionaire" you don't have to know anything—other than how to say "That's my final answer"—to take advantage of the game's favorable gambling opportunities. You just have to have the heart (and wisdom) to know you're doing the right thing.

Now, those who *do* know something do, of course, enjoy a great advantage. A photographic memory and an insatiable appetite for learning otherwise useless esoterica comes in handy on this show. But equally important is approaching the game as if it were a gambling tournament, where the money must be thought of merely as "chips" and each decision made must be considered solely in terms of expected value. If the answer to the show's eponymous rhetorical question is indeed "everyone," then contestants would do well to think more like wiseguy gamblers and less like degenerate slot machine junkies.

Gambling Around The World 13

Gambling.

That word, that one word, does something to people. *Gambling.* It makes you excited or angry or sad or elated or whatever—but it means *something* to you. It recalls an unforgettable anecdote, a thrilling triumph, a crushing defeat. It suggests romance and danger and, naturally, risk and reward. It means engaging life—sometimes courageously, sometimes foolishly—and not seeking refuge in the safe and the secure.

Taking a chance.

To succeed, to really succeed, you've got to take chances. One does not enjoy the fruits of success without making some calculated gambles along the way, whether in business, love, or for that matter, any part of being alive.

Formalized places to take chances—casinos—can be found in every part of the world. And though the games and odds vary little wherever you gamble, not all casinos are created equal. The rows of slot machines may sound the same and the green baize of the blackjack table may look identical no matter what continent it stands upon, but few casinos *feel* the same. It's the old form-and-content issue: Most gambling joints contain a similar commodity (games of chance whose odds are skewed in the house's favor), but the exceptional ones—the ones I prefer to visit—present their product in a rare and inspiring way.

You'll find these special places scattered throughout the world, from Europe and North America to the Caribbean and Asia. And while I cannot guarantee that you'll depart any of these casinos a winner—in fact, you're much more likely to leave a loser—I'm confident you'll be glad that you went. For these are, in my estimation, some of the best places in the world to take a gamble.

Atlantis, Paradise Island, Bahamas

The phrases "first-class casino" and "Samuel Taylor Coleridge's *Rime of the Ancient Mariner*" do not often appear in the same sentence. Which is one reason why Atlantis, the newest, largest, and loveliest casino in the Caribbean, deserves a visit. There is indeed "water, water everywhere" on this themed property. And while you'll find plenty of it to drink—with 32 restaurants and 18 lounges, thirst is not an issue—the majority of the eight million gallons of water at Atlantis are contained in a 21-foot-deep lagoon, representing the "ruins" of Poseidon's mythical lost city. In this lagoon, bordered by five-inch-thick see-through acrylic, 13,000 creatures of the sea make their graceful peripatetic journeys, including stingrays, lobsters, groupers, tuna, sharks, and all manner of phosphorescent tropical fish, glowing with hallucinogenic colors that appear nowhere else in nature.

Forget faux volcanoes and fighting pirate ships and lazy white tigers: This aquarium is the greatest hotel-casino attraction on Earth.

Atlantis is a half-billion-dollar attempt to recreate mythology, albeit in polished marble and gold leaf. The place "drips"—in luxury. A 2,500-square-foot "bridge suite," connecting two hotel towers, can host a single high roller or a party of 200; it's yours for $25,000 a night. Much of the sprawling resort's architecture seems to rise majestically from the water, and the enormous pool complex— an amalgam of baths, lagoons, and ocean—affords guests the aquatic options of luxuriating, exercising, or subjecting themselves to abject terror. The latter manifests in the form of a waterslide known as the "Leap of Faith," which plunges riders downward at 37 mph—through a shark tank.

The really pungent danger, of course, comes in the casino, which is easily the prettiest in the Caribbean. Aquatic-themed glass sculptures that hang from above and floor-to-ceiling windows (a rarity in casinos anywhere) showcase the ravishing seas beyond Atlantis' shores. It's a gorgeous place. But like the Sirens of myth, the casino can be a cruel seductress. The odds on most of Atlantis' games range from average (roulette, blackjack) to downright poor (video poker machines that pay out below 95%; Caribbean Stud tables that offer a meager $55,000 jackpot). All of which reminds you once again of the Poseidon story this whole fabulous joint is based on: Atlantis was finally done in by rampant money hunger.

Atlantis is not merely a casino that happens to have a hotel attached to it. It is a world-class resort that sits beside a casino.

Casino Baden-Baden, Baden-Baden, Germany

This is one of the few casinos in the world where men attired in tuxedos won't feel overdressed.

The theme here, like the town of Baden-Baden itself, is Old World Elegance. Imagine a building that mixes a Venetian *palazzo* with New York's Frick Museum and the public rooms at Versailles. Now put some roulette tables beneath the towering ceilings. What you have here is an atmosphere of such heightened refinement that the absence of scantily clad cocktail waitresses bearing free drinks seems not an oversight but a blessing. If you're a man eager to play James Bond for one night or a woman eager to reincarnate Marlene Deitrich (who called this place the most beautiful casino in all of Europe), the Casino Baden-Baden provides a convincing setting.

The decorative vitrines here aren't just nice porcelain thingies; they're Ming vases. The paintings on the ceiling aren't merely the interior designer's afterthoughts; they're Renaissance frescoes. There's gold and crushed velvet and big overstuffed divans everywhere.

Which is all to say you don't see this kind of gambling den in the state of New Jersey.

A perfect Baden-Baden day might go something like this. After arriving in Frankfurt, experience the exhilarating freedom of the Autobahn. (Preferably in a really fast German car.) Upon arrival in Baden-Baden, head straight for the Brenner's Park Hotel, another paragon of Old World Elegance, and, burrito-like, enjoy a seaweed-wrap "jet-lag treatment"; take the curative waters at the Friedrichspad, a public bath in the center of town; stroll among Baden-Baden's quiet lanes and beside the River Oos; return to Brenner's Park for a massage and facial, administered by a pretty young *fraulein*; retire to your sprawling suite to recover from the unremitting relaxation; dine with your lovely companion in the hotel's unremittingly elegant restaurant; win piles of money at the unremittingly elegant casino.

That last part, actually, might be a bit difficult. The surroundings at Casino Baden-Baden are sublime, but the games of chance are limited and not particularly attractive. Though poker is dealt on the weekends, during the week nearly every table at Casino Baden-Baden is devoted to roulette—albeit the European single-zero variety, which is roughly twice as good a gamble as the double-zero American type, but still a losing proposition. On a recent visit, I saw but one table open for baccarat and one for blackjack (with pernicious rules that grossly favor the house); every other table was devoted to the spinning ball.

And yet one feels strangely privileged to lose here. There's a small admission charge and a jacket and tie are required. (The porters have a closet full of fashion relics for visitors who come unprepared.) The crowd is handsome and speaks many languages. Urbanity and sophistication (and the smoke of Cuban cigars) suffuse the air. And somehow, thanks to the magic of a bygone time perhaps, you've become Sean Connery.

The Ritz Club, London, England

The Sultan of a Certain Asian Island; Australia's Leading Real Estate Tycoon; That Middle Eastern Arms Dealer Gentleman—these are some of the Ritz Club's clientele. And you can be a client, too, whether you make headlines or not.

The easiest way to get in, as with most private clubs, is through a member's introduction. Here's another way: If you're staying at the famously refined hotel above the casino, you will almost certainly be admitted. Membership usually costs 500 pounds, but this will typically be waived for "the right type" of person. (And you know who you are.) Thanks to Byzantine British rules and regulations meant to weed out the "unwanted element," prospective punters must endure a 24-hour waiting period before they can start to "game," as the euphemism goes. Once you have received your security clearance, you enjoy all the privileges of membership.

And it is a privilege. The Ritz Club is a beautiful place, fine and rich in every way, but restrained enough by good British taste to pull up safely short of overdone. There is much gold and chintz and lead glass, but the lighting is subdued and the colors muted; you feel as though you are inhabiting a painting by, say, Fragonard or Watteau, only without the pouffy wigs and apple-blush cheeks.

Again because of strict regulations, casinos in London cannot offer their prized customers some of the same complimentary perquisites that are staples of the Las Vegas high-roller scene: no free airfare or penthouse hotel suites or fight tickets allowed. But the casinos are permitted to buy guests dinner on premises. Thus, armed with a budget other casinos pour into chartered jets, the restaurant here is among the finest in all of England, with a wine list that doesn't skimp on first-growth clarets and a menu that does not want for anything. Catering to a truly international clientele, the Ritz Club restaurant offers everything from Lebanese to Thai to Italian cuisine, and it's all good. (If what you want somehow isn't on the encyclopedic menu, they'll make it for you.) Dining here is alone worth becoming a member.

The gambling area is a cozy quiet ballroom, with Frank Sinatra and Ella Fitzgerald supplanting the usual drone of slot machines. Indeed, you won't find machines of any sort here, nor will you see a dice game. That, you see, would be too loud, and not really the kind of thing this sort of club goes in for, old boy. Otherwise, all the usual suspects—roulette, punto banco (baccarat), blackjack—are readily available, with minimum bets commensurate with the membership's net worth. The 21 game at the Ritz Club is quite decent and worth playing, though there are a few peculiar rules and regulations—decreed, of course, by the government—that are meant to protect players but, in fact, hurt them slightly.

The pain passes quickly. Note the grand crystal chandeliers, the wood-trimmed gaming tables, the pretty dealers in *dresses*—you'd be hard-pressed to find a lovelier place than the Ritz Club to take a chance.

Casino Lisboa, Macau

Let's be perfectly clear: There is nothing remotely elegant about gambling in Macau, a small formerly Portuguese-controlled island off the coast of China, near Hong Kong. There is nothing remotely refined or lovely or beautiful about the casinos here. There is nothing charming. Indeed, casinos in Macau are positively grungy, with harsh light, grating noise, and alarming signs on the walls imploring patrons to exercise proper hygiene.

What's wonderful about gambling in Macau is the energy, the manic preposterously charged energy of making a wager among some of the most gambling-crazed bettors on Earth. Visiting a casino in Macau is like going to a bullfight—except in Macau you're viewing the mayhem from the middle of the ring.

The most chaotic of the dozen or so gambling dens on the island is the Casino Lisboa, a six-story monument to risk-reward frenzy, in which the limits (and prospective fortunes) rise on each succeeding floor. Except for the horse-racing tracks of Hong Kong—themselves an hour away by hydrofoil—there's probably no place on Earth where more money is won or lost per hour. (The New York Stock Exchange doesn't count). The clientele here, which is almost exclusively Chinese, has a fanatical compulsion to wager as much of their net worth as possible on the turn of a card or the tumble of a die and, thus, they're not shy about letting their allegiances and passions be known. (Curses and hexes and other shouts of encouragement tend to fill the air.) The atmosphere at Casino Lisboa is theatrically loud, the emotions theatrically large, and the results predictably dramatic.

Imagine earning $50,000 a year and having $50,000 or more riding on a hand of baccarat and you might sympathize with the alternately stricken and triumphant protagonists who populate this place.

The Casino Lisboa is not the loveliest place in the world to gamble. But it's certainly one of the most entertaining.

Caesars Palace, Las Vegas, Nevada

Taken as a whole, as a sprawling collection of iniquitous dens of depravity, there is no finer gambling destination in the world than Las Vegas. The plethora of casinos breeds competition, which, sage economists have taught us, in turn breeds the best product at the best price. Therefore, in the middle of the Mojave Desert, far from any sign of civilization other than three-story-tall marquees advertising $4.95 prime rib, gamblers enjoy the fairest bets in all the world. Nowhere do video poker machines pay out better than Las Vegas. Nowhere are there better blackjack games. Nowhere are jackpots higher, choices wider, or tariffs lighter.

It's the best place on the planet to gamble.

And of all the beautiful, exciting, surreal casinos in Sin City, there is no place in Las Vegas I more enjoy gambling than at Caesars Palace.

The Roman "theme" is by now a tired conceit, original in its day, but more likely to inspire giggles at present, especially when mighty Caesar and his lovely Cleopatra stroll past a bank of slot machines with a muscular centurion and a fair maiden strewing rose petals in their path. Yet there is still something captivating about entering this "empire." The place pulses with the seductive energy of sex and power, with the allure of millions won and lost. While Caesars Palace has made some cursory nods toward the "family market" in the form of an IMAX theater and a modest video arcade, the casino remains the domain of the adult—specifically, the high roller.

And Caesars Palace certainly knows how to cater to the high roller's whims. The restaurants here are, as a group, among the best in the city. The accommodations rival those of any five-star brand—though you may safely assume if Ritz-Carlton ran Caesars Palace, it wouldn't provide mirrors over the beds. And the hotel, dining, and casino staff are all well-versed in service, courtesy, and exceeding expectations.

The betting limits are among the highest in Las Vegas; indeed, Caesars Palace was for many years one of the few places left in Nevada where a serious bettor could wager what he wished on a sporting event. (Until they merged with the Hilton chain, Caesars Palace had the best sports book in town by far.) The blackjack games are plentiful and fair. The crap tables are always buzzing with chip-stacking action. And if you fancy roulette, management will gladly reserve a single-zero table for you in the Olympic Casino before, during, or after the heavyweight title fight.

Even with the arrival of many highly touted newcomers, Caesars Palace is still my favorite hotel-casino in Las Vegas, a magical site that offers all the latest pleasures without forgetting the charms of Vegas past. In that regard, Caesars Palace is one of the few "sure things" in the unpredictable world of gambling.

Telling Lies and Getting Paid

Jes drinkin' and gamblin', boys," he says, laying down his cards. "Drinkin' and gamblin'! Evuh day's a party and evuh night's a Saturday night!"

He's got the "nuts," the unbeatable lock hand, a hand he wasn't supposed to have—and he's letting the other nine players at our poker table know it. "Gimme that money, honey!" he implores the dealer. "I'm jes a po' boy from Texas and I need as much money as I can git." Raymond—that's what we'll call him—is one of the most successful bookies in Houston. He doesn't need the $600 pile of poker chips the dealer, inevitably, shoves his way. (His organization clears more than $100,000 a week; winning or losing $600 concerns him about as much as it would you or me if a quarter fell through a hole in our pocket.) Indeed, the $600 in chips is not even worth $600. It's tournament money, a bunch of tokens. Still, Raymond intends to crow long and loud enough that his opponents get sufficiently fed up with him to do something stupid.

It's 1992. I'm playing with Ray and a school of other

sharks in a satellite tournament at the World Series of Poker at Binion's Horseshoe in downtown Las Vegas.

The main event, the World Championship, is a grueling four-day affair that costs $10,000 to enter. Some competitors, such as two-time World Champions Johnny Chan and Doyle Brunson, are too busy playing in side games laden with $1,000 chips—real $1,000 chips—to waste time dabbling in satellite tournaments. But for working stiffs like me, satellites are mandatory. The PGA Tour has them, and so does the tennis circuit. For those without full-time playing privileges, these golf and tennis mini-tournaments are a weekly odyssey. The winner of the satellite earns a coveted spot in the big show. It's the same at the World Series of Poker. The Horseshoe conducts daily $220-buy-in tournaments that award winners a $10,000 seat in the World Championship. The losers watch on television. Or get press credentials.

I've played in dozens of satellites leading up to my 1992 campaign, winning a few minor events and finishing in the money (the final table) at some major ones. But I've never won a satellite for the Big One, the World Series of Poker main event. For years I've *written* about the championship, enjoying intimate access to the greatest tournament poker players on Earth, observing the insights and judgments and character that place these wizards on a slightly elevated plane, a place where studying and reading (and writing) about the game are woeful substitutes for talent and experience. Years of chronicling the exploits of the best players in the game have afforded me the kind of training a young lad earned in the Middle Ages when he served as an unpaid and much-abused apprentice to, say, a pedophilic blacksmith.

Thanks to my assignments as an ink-stained wretch, I've effectively been mentored in the game of poker, though my mentors are blissfully unaware that they've taught me anything—except perhaps how to give a thoroughly uninteresting interview filled with a litany of clichés. (Most great poker players—as with most great artists—have difficulty articulating how they do what they do; they just do.) Armed with what I take to be an unimpeachably authoritative compendium of poker knowledge, I figure I'm ready to cross the threshold from voyeur to participant. If I can win my way into the main event, I'll know I deserve to play with the big boys. Thus far I haven't deserved it. Tonight, though, I'm seated with a bunch of fools like Raymond, and I've got a terrific chance.

We're down to 27 players. The top three will all win $10,000 seats in the main event; fourth, fifth, and sixth will earn several thousand dollars, and the remaining three at the final table will pocket several hundred. I'm feeling good.

Mine is one of those dream tables you sometimes encounter in Las Vegas, a collection of players who, lacking skill, compensate with outlandish theatrics. Dueling Raymond for the title of Loudest Voice is Jimmy, who raises fighting cocks outside of Lafayette, Louisiana. All week, Jimmy, who looks to be in his fifties, has garnered the admiration of his opponents by having two fetching teenage girls—one blonde, one brunette—accompany his every move, like a couple of Cajun geishas. When he makes an ill-advised bluff and gets raised, Jimmy turns to his girls and proclaims in a Creole growl, "I make a bet, *everyone* call me. Shit, guy at the next table call me! Guy across the street pick up the phone and call me!" His girls titter respectfully and return to preening.

Billy's at my table, too. He runs a gun shop in Alabama. Someone asks him how's business. "Bettuh'n evuh," drawls Billy. "Evuh-budy got *someone* they wanna kill." I tell myself that even if I fail to place in this satellite tournament, my cash investment has bought me an evening worthy of *Guys and Dolls*. What a cast! The Jew

Boy writer and a chorus of redneck Bubbas. Earlier in the tourney, our table disposed of a 450-pound guy named Oklahoma Bob, owner of a port-a-potty concern. His baseball cap, tilted rakishly on his balding crown, proclaimed him to be "Number One in the Number Two Business!"

Across from the empty space that Bob's gargantuan girth previously occupied sits a taciturn enigma named John, whose dyed-black perm, smoky sunglasses, and necklaces entwined in chest hair recall a disco-era wild and crazy guy. Despite a gold-chunk bracelet around one wrist and diamond-encrusted watch around the other, John takes a distant second in the over-accessorized department. That honor easily goes to the gentleman on my left, Ed, who sports sparkling diamond rings *on every finger of both hands.*

Ray continues to yell about drinking and gambling. Jimmy is sending one of his under-aged ladies-in-waiting for an antacid. Ed is clipping his manicured nails. John has a few chips left. Billy is surveying the room, seeing if he can outlast 18 more players. And I look down and see my poker dreams have come true.

Aces in the hole.

It's become a mythic phrase applied to any situation where hidden power lurks, where a secret weapon waits to be unleashed. In almost any poker game—seven-stud, five-card draw—aces in the hole are strong. In no-limit Texas hold 'em , the game we're playing now, aces in the hole is the most powerful hand you can possibly start with. (Hold 'em is played with two hole cards and five "community" cards. Players make the best five-card poker hand from the quintet of "up" cards and the duo of "down" cards. "No limit" means just that—you can bet all of your chips at any time.) Like Stanley Cups in New York and pennants in Chicago, pocket aces show up with depressing infrequency, only .45% of the time,

142

one in every 220 hands, or about once in every six hours of continuous betting, raising, and folding.

Not only do I have wired aces, I'm on the "button," the last player to act. With nine people before me, chances are good that someone will raise the pot, either because he's bluffing or because he has a legitimately strong hand. I'm hoping someone will make a large bet, which I can then re-raise. *Please!* I'm screaming in my head, *someone raise this pot!*

During the eternal 10 seconds it takes for betting to commence, I glance around the room: three tables left in the satellite; my birthday numbers up on the keno board; Doyle Brunson, playing with Chan, one table over in the corner, scooping up a pot larger than most people's yearly income. Doyle's book, *Super/System*, is the poker-player's bible, a 605-page repository of secrets that every fledgling card sharp commits to memory. One of Brunson's maxims, buried in the chapter on no-limit Texas hold 'em, goes like this: "Most of the time, a pair of aces in the hole will either win you a small pot or lose you a big one." I'm displeased to remember that lesson at this particular moment.

In early position, Billy raises the antes $400. *(Yes!)* Everyone folds until it comes around to Raymond, who's grown unusually circumspect. He scratches his beard, looks at Billy, and re-raises $1,200. *(Yes!!)* John folds. Jimmy folds. It's up to me. I don't want to put on too much of a show, but I don't want to act too quickly either. I want to suggest uncertainty, even though I'm completely certain of what I must do. I peek at my hole cards, look at the pot, scan my stack of chips, and deadpan, "Raise." I match Raymond's $1,600 and shove $2,200 more—all my money—toward the center. "All in," announces the dealer.

Billy sighs and folds without hesitation. Raymond stares at me glumly. "You got somethin' there, writer boy?" he asks, riffling chips between his long fingers. I stare beyond him, at Doyle Brunson. "I'm gonna have to call you," Raymond snarls. *(Yes!!!)* He puts in nearly all his chips. The pot has swelled to more than $8,000. Winning it will virtually guarantee me a spot at the final table and an odds-on shot at grabbing my first seat at the $10,000 World Championship.

"You got a pair?" Raymond asks me weakly. I nod confidently. "Shit," he groans, turning over two little deuces. "I was hoping you had ace-king or something." I show him my two aces, and he nods. "Shit." He knows the probabilities, and they're the poker equivalent of having Shaquille O'Neal posted up on Mugsy Bogues: The only card that can help him now is a deuce, and only two remain in the deck. I'm close to a 5-1 favorite. The dealer flops the first three community cards: six-nine-king of various suits. He turns the next card, "fourth street." Another six. Only one card, "the river," remains. One card between me and poker nirvana.

It's a deuce.

"How 'bout that!" Raymond yelps, gathering in the spoils of his improbable full house. I try unsuccessfully to force a smile and wish everyone luck, but my face feels frozen, as though the fateful deuce has splashed a large puddle of novocaine onto my cheeks. I'm speechless. I'm catatonic. I'm done.

As I depart, hoping I'll make it back to my room before I start whimpering, Doyle Brunson glances my way. The dealer at his table is pushing Johnny Chan a pot that appears to have nearly $100,000 of Doyle's money in it. Brunson, the old master, sits placidly, unmoved. His expression is blank, unreadable. I briefly consider telling him about my $8,000 bad beat, about his aces-in-the-hole maxim getting proven one more ugly time. But I sense this might not be the best moment.

Doyle Brunson reaches into a black shoulder bag and

pulls out $75,000 more to play with. I walk past the Horseshoe's Gallery of Champions, a pantheon of the World Series of Poker's past winners, and trudge off toward the nickel slots.

For six more years I write about the World Series of Poker, the world's greatest gambling tournament, where, in the World Championship main event, players put up $10,000 each and play until one person has all the chips. And a $1 million cash prize. I play in poker tournaments around the world, events you've probably never heard of, losing many, placing in the money in some, and winning a few. Like the minor-league baseball prospect who has just enough success at Double A ball to think he might get a crack at the Big Leagues, I win enough (and learn enough) to think I might one day be worthy of a shot at the Main Event. Every year I trek to Binion's Horseshoe and, pen in hand, dutifully note the exploits of the world's best poker players. And with every passing year, I come closer to convincing myself that I'm one of them—that I should be huddled with the living legends of the game, the Johnny Chans and Stu Ungars and Doyle Brunsons, betting, raising, and folding in quest of the most revered prize in poker.

But I've always had this rule: If you can't win your way in, you're not good enough to compete. Fact is, anyone who wants to play in the Main Event can simply plunk down $10,000 cash and take a seat, and every year about a third of the field does. But the majority of players, me included, play in satellites. Granted, these are numerical longshots—typically 200 or more players vying for a few spots—but every night during the three weeks leading up to the Main Event, someone converts a $220 entry fee into an invitation to the big dance. Satellites are difficult to win, terribly difficult, but if you do beat the long odds, you've instantly created for yourself an overlay, a situation in which your long-term expectation is greater than the equity you've invested. Indeed, to play in a $10,000-buy-in poker tournament for a few hundred dollars is about as big of an overlay as you'll ever find inside a casino.

On the night in 1998 that I arrive at the Horseshoe, five days before the Main Event, I play in the first of what I expect will be many satellite tournaments. Thanks to sharp play, good judgment and, it must be said, some extraordinarily good luck, my first satellite tournament of the 1998 World Series of Poker is my last. Eight hours after I arrive in Las Vegas, I've won a seat in the Main Event.

As the final hand is dealt, eliminating the last player standing between me and my poker dream-come-true, I sit dumbly in my chair, staring blankly at the dealer. All around me there is much hooting and hollering and back-slapping. But I am stunned. Because I realize: In five days I'm going to be playing for the World Championship of Poker. And then I do something you should never do at a poker table: I cry.

Like a boxer preparing for the ring, I spend the next few days getting ready. But instead of road work and hours on the heavy bag, I review oft-read poker text-books, play a few more satellite tourneys down the street at the Plaza (winning again!), and conduct a feverish internal debate with myself over the importance of having lucky talismans wedged in my pocket when the Main Event begins. Look, I'm a long-time gambling writer; I know holding onto locks of hair from my dog, cat, and girlfriend will have absolutely no effect whatsoever on the cards I am dealt. I know!

But I figure, what the hell. They can't hurt.

The morning of the World Championship, I rise early and complete what is supposed to be an hour-long jog in twenty minutes. I eat about four bites of what is supposed to be a nourishing fruit-plate breakfast. My digestive system is not working well.

You might say I'm nervous.

What worries me most, I come to understand after an impromptu therapy session with my girlfriend, is failure. Not the failure of losing the $1 million—or, for that matter, the $697,000 second prize, or $25,000 27th prize—but of failing to play well. I'm scared of playing like an idiot, of giving my chips away like a hopeless old lady in thrall to a televangelist. I'm scared of not belonging in this competition—and scared that my play will confirm my fears.

An hour before game time, I'm laying in my hotel bed, with the shades drawn, silently reassuring myself that the only way I can fail is if I don't enjoy myself.

It works. I feel swell. I'm ready. Only problem is, so immersed am I in deep-breathing exercises, positive visualization, and various other affirming rituals I'm too embarrassed to describe, I arrive late, missing the tournament's first two hands and the poker equivalent of "Gentlemen, start your engines!": Tournament Coordinator Jack McClelland's famous direction of "Shuffle-up and deal!"

When I float in, carried along on a buoyant current of newfound equanimity, the scene is electric, pulsing with a potent mixture of anticipation and dread. Four days from now, someone, one of the 350 players congregated at Binion's Horseshoe, will be crowned the World Champion of Poker. Someone will have survived.

Everyone else will have perished. This accident scene waiting to happen draws a large crowd of onlookers, a menagerie of media types, curious bystanders taking a break from the slot machines, and legions of crestfallen poker players who didn't make it into the field. I know how they feel, because for many years I stood exactly where they stand, wishing I were inside the ropes, not outside looking in.

Dashing to Table 50, I take my seat—the 8-seat, two to the dealer's right—check that my $10,000 stake is intact, and look around to get my bearings. Matt Damon, doing publicity for his upcoming poker movie and, thus, surrounded by a swarm of television cameras, is two tables away. The legendary Doyle Brunson is at Damon's table, waiting to suck in his loose movie-star money. Huck Seed, a former World Champion I've previously written about, is at a table over my left shoulder, as is Berry Johnston, another all-time-great former titleholder.

And at my table, the only table in the universe that matters to me, starting now, are the eight other fellows with whom I hope to be spending the next eight hours. I've played with all but two of these guys, and none of them are soft. There aren't any World Champions here, but several of the players have come breathlessly close. In the 2-seat is John Spadevecchia, who finished third three years ago; next to him is Hans "Tuna" Lund, who has finished second in the Main Event and first in numerous other poker tournaments; and beside the big fish is my friend Blair Rodman, a fierce competitor who finished high in the money last year, and who, coincidentally, played golf with me two days earlier. But there will be no "gimmes" today.

My game plan—to fold *everything* for the first hour unless I'm dealt aces, kings, queens, or ace-king—becomes obsolete within five minutes. Like a hound on the scent of a squirrel, I can't contradict my instincts. My poker conditioning has become so acute that when I see a good opportunity to "pick up" (or steal) a tiny pot, I pounce—like that old hound. That I have nothing worth playing in my hand doesn't make any difference. My position—last of the players to act—is perfect, and based on the betting and body language of my opponents, I can sense, I'm *certain*, nobody is going to call my modest raise. The fear I thought might cripple me, the kind of fear that paralyzes and robs sound judgment, never materializes. I had envisioned myself hyperventilating the first time I tried to play a pot in the World Championship, like a fledgling actor gripped with stage fright, but when I say "raise" and toss my chips into the pot, it feels just like any other of the hundreds of poker tournaments I've played in. My life is on a weird tape-delay at the moment. A few seconds later, when I fully realize how much is at stake, I get way too nervous to make the raise. Fortunately, it's already in the recent past.

Everybody folds, the dealer pushes me the pot, and, simple as that, I'm no longer a World Series of Poker virgin. I've won my first pot on the eighth hand of the tournament. And my heart did not suffer any unusual palpitations. My palms did not start secreting a cold viscous liquid. I did not soil myself. Everything is fine. Now I can play.

For the next 90 minutes, I build up to $11,400 without ever having a showdown. A little pot here, a minor bluff there—no major confrontations, no high drama. Just solid positional poker—the kind that can get you in the money, yet seldom wins first place. For now, though, that will do nicely. I'm just relieved not to have made a premature exit. I want to live a little before I die.

At the end of the first level, several big name professionals are out, including the brilliant Phil Hellmuth, Jr., another of my profile subjects, a man of whom I have written admiringly in the past. How strange—how wonderful, I must admit—to be in the running while he's not. I feel like a young boy who has just discovered, after many years of practice and instruction, that he can finally drive his golf ball past his dad. I feel like I belong here.

The "blind" bets—a form of anteing—double in size at the second level, as they will continue to do for the rest of the tournament. Steadily escalating stakes means you *have* to play; you can't merely sit and wait to be dealt miracle cards. But you can't be reckless, either. Success in any poker tournament, especially the World Series of Poker, is contingent on many factors—skill, timing, luck—but the key element may be picking your spots, engaging in big confrontations selectively and, unless you know you have way the best of the battle, rarely.

During the tournament's second level, almost three-and-a-half hours after the first hand has been dealt, I still haven't shown down a single hand. That is to say, I haven't turned over my cards once! Yet I've managed to build my bankroll to a healthy $15,000, mainly by betting aggressively when I'm committed to a hand and folding it when I'm not. No raising wars, no final-card heroics—just solid well-modulated poker. The largest pot I win, about $1,800, comes to me when my opponent, Spadevecchia, who had called a series of raises before and after the flop, decides he can't call my $2,000 bet on the end.

Almost concurrent with my emerging belief that I'm playing wonderfully well, I make two big blunders and blow off a big chunk of chips. Twice I lead at a flop, get called, and lead again, only to be raised. Two bad bluffs and I'm back down to $7,800.

Immediately returning to form, I grind my way back up to $12,400, never showing down a hand. After four hours of play, nearly 100 contestants have already been eliminated. The 250 or so of us that remain should now have proportionally more chips among us. In a poker tournament, you need to be like a whale swimming through an ocean of plankton, slurping up as many chips as you can get your jaws around. Paul "Eskimo" Clark, a top tournament player who, as you might imagine, looks like an Alaskan Inuit, is the king of the Arctic at this point. Every time I turn around to check the tables behind me, his stack of chips has grown another inch or two. The $45,000 or so he's accumulated makes my wee twelve-and-change feel like a country cottage compared to his burgeoning skyscraper.

During the next two hours, the third level, I play poker about as well as I ever have. Without putting too many of my chips at risk, yet betting aggressively enough to shake the confidence of my opponents, I steadily build to $18,600 in chips without losing a hand. My competitors, I can feel, are starting to fear and respect me—the ideal result, according to my United States Marine Corps upbringing. After six hours, I know I can play with anyone at my table, including the almost-World Champions.

And even better, I can see they know it, too.

At the fourth level, we're playing with $100 and $200 blind bets, as well as a compulsory $25 ante, and contestants are starting to drop out quickly. The field is down to 225 or so, and our table has already had its share of victims. Each time someone gets eliminated, tables are consolidated and another player is brought in to fill the seat. (Sometimes two players in a row get eliminated from the same seat; it then becomes known as "the electric chair.") When the player to my immediate left loses the last of his chips, a new kid comes to town, taking the empty seat. And that's when the trouble begins.

I know the man—his name is Larry—since I've played in many tournaments with him. But I can't remember his style of play—if he's a loose cannon or as tight as a miser. I can't recall if he can be induced into making bad calls or if he's impossible to bluff. He's a cipher.

Ideally, I'd like to watch Larry for a few rounds. But two hands after he sits down, before I can get a line on his play, I'm dealt the best cards I've seen since the World Series of Poker Main Event began. I peek at my pair of red kings, and I know I've got to play.

I'm first to act—"one off the blinds," in poker parlance—and I raise the pot $600, requiring anyone who wants to play his hand to put in $800. Larry, the next to act, pauses momentarily and, to my surprise, calls. Everyone else folds.

Unless he has aces—and I don't think he does, or else he probably would have re-raised me—I've got the best hand before the flop. I figure him for something like ace-king, possibly of the same suit. As long as the dealer doesn't put an ace on the board, I figure I'm good.

The flop comes 10-6-4, with two hearts. It's a flop I like. Not wanting to give my opponent a "free" card, a chance to improve his hand at no cost, I bet $1,600.

Larry thinks for a moment, looks at his pile of $24,000 in chips, and says, "I raise." He matches my $1,600 bet and puts another $3,000 in the pot.

Before I do any analysis, my first instinct is to fold. There's an old saying in poker: "If you can't sometimes fold the best hand, you'll never be a winner." I think I probably have the best hand—but I'm not sure. And given my position (first to act), Larry can exploit my uncertainty. I have about $18,000 in front of me. I can fold, accept my $2,400 loss and live to fight another battle, when I'm sure of where I stand.

But. Yet. However ... This is the best hand I've seen in more than seven hours of poker. I may have Larry drawing dead to two or three cards, making me a big favorite to take down a monster pot. On the other hand. …

I run through the possibilities.

— He has aces, which he slow-played before the flop, hoping I would bet out: *Possible, but unlikely.*

— He has a flush draw, ace-queen of hearts maybe, and he's running what's called a semi-bluff, raising with the worst hand, but knowing it can improve to the best hand if called: *Possible. But very courageous.*

— He has three-of-a-kind and wants to shut me out of the pot in case I have the flush draw: *Could it be? Would he call my raise from early position with a pair of fours, sixes, or tens? Possibly. But if he has indeed flopped trips, wouldn't he merely want to call and let me blow off more money on the next round? If I knew my man better, I could make a better decision.*

— He has the same hand as me, kings, and he's exploiting his superior position: *Highly improbable.*

— He has queens or jacks and thinks he has the best hand: *Were it so! But probably not.*

— He has nothing (a small pair, perhaps) and is running a stone-cold bluff: *Only one way to find out.*

I mull my options. Fold or raise; fold or raise. I don't even consider calling, since, if any card but a king falls on fourth street, I'm stuck in the same uncertain predicament. (One professional gambler friend of mine thinks calling the $3,000 would have been a great play, for reasons that are too esoteric for my meager poker intelligence.) To me, the decision is clear: Either fold or raise.

I can't decide. I just don't know.

For two minutes I think. (Two minutes is an eternity at the poker table.) I stare at Larry, trying to get a hint from his body language. He's still and silent, and he doesn't respond when I talk to him. "If you've got aces, you've got me beat," I say, seeing if he'll react. He doesn't.

I don't know. I look around the table. The rest of the

153

group is growing impatient, yet nobody says anything. They sense the gravity of the moment.

I decide to raise.

Now, "decide" is not really the word, since I'm not at all convinced that this is the correct move. But I'm having something akin to an out-of-body experience: My mouth is saying "raise" and my hands are putting another $8,000 in chips into the pot. Yet my heart is not remotely convinced that my hands and mouth know what they're doing. I'm watching a film of myself, and I am powerless to change the ending.

Larry considers my bet for about three seconds and moves all his chips into the pot. "All in," he says, raising me another $10,000 or so.

I shake my head in disgust and flip my kings into the muck.

"I guess I should have just folded after the first bet," I say ruefully to Blair, at the other end of the table.

"I smelled trips," he says. I nod disconsolately. Larry, busy stacking up what used to be mine, has no comment.

I've lost $10,400 on one hand, my entire profit after nearly seven-and-a-half-hours of tournament poker. I'm back down to $10,000.

And I'm officially on tilt.

It doesn't take me long to blow off what remains of my bankroll. I run two horribly unsuccessful bluffs against the only two players at the table on whom a bluff isn't going to work. In other words, I try to get fancy with a couple of donkeys.

That costs me another $5,000 or so.

And then, twenty minutes later, I pick up a moderately good hand, ace-queen of diamonds, in early position and, not thinking about lasting until the second day, not thinking about collecting myself and recouping the chips I've given away, not thinking about much of anything, I raise all-in.

This is a terrifically stupid play, since the only hands that will call me are hands that can beat me. And sure enough, a quiet fellow who hasn't played anything all day calls me with aces. Thirty seconds later, I'm out of the 1998 World Series of Poker.

I spend the next few hours—okay, the next few days— filled with self-loathing and regret. Failing to win, to place in the money, to even make the second day wouldn't bother me so much if I had merely gotten unlucky. That happens; it's a cruel part of poker. What hurts is knowing I played so well, so beautifully, then managed to play so rottenly. I—not fate, not Lady Luck, not any other euphemistic apparition—am the reason I was eliminated from the World Series of Poker. And for that I am profoundly disappointed.

For weeks, I have nightmares about my big hand with Larry. I literally wake up in the middle of the night, reliving the pot as if it were a fiery plane crash. Almost every day I torture myself (and my friends) recounting the ominous events. I talk about the hand endlessly with my poker pals, and I always come to the same conclusion: I played the hand badly, really badly.

It starts to consume me. I even suggest to my girlfriend that I might get Larry's telephone number from the Horseshoe and give him a call, tell him I'm writing a story, and, you know, would he mind telling me, for the sake of journalism, what he had?

But eventually I come to my senses. And I'm consoled by a simple realization: There will be another World Series of Poker next year. And the next. And I will only get better. As in life, there will be some poker decisions I'll regret and some I'll rejoice, some memories I'll loathe and some I'll cherish. And, like life, the game will go on and on, making heroes and fools out of us all, long after I've stopped playing.

My equanimity and wisdom last for about two days. Like a jilted suitor, I brood for many months over the One That Got Away. This is not to say I obsess about my missed opportunity at the 1998 World Series of Poker on a daily basis—only weekly. After several months of "beating myself up," as the 12-step crowd is fond of saying, I eventually realize the general unhealthiness—not to mention silliness—of fixating on a poker tournament I never came close to winning.

But instead of seeking psychoanalytic counseling and various serotonin-affecting medications, I launch a new strategy: Play as many no-limit tournaments as time permits, and condition myself into a better, more infallible, player, like a boxer preparing for a fight. My inspiration is something Oscar de la Hoya told me when I interviewed him one day during a friendly round of golf. "When you're in the best shape of your life," the welterweight champ counseled, "you feel like nothing can hurt you. You can get hit with the other guy's best shot, and you don't even feel it. It's like you're invincible."

In my quest to possess something like poker invincibility, I play and study and think and play and analyze and play and play some more. And between the conclusion of the 1998 World Series of Poker and the weeks leading up to the 1999 World Series of Poker, I finish at the final table of more than 50% of the 16 no-limit tournaments I enter. This may be some sort of record, and if it isn't, it ought to be. It's a record for me, certainly. I tell my friend C, a superb tournament player who has fin- ished in the money several times at the World Champion- ship, that I'm playing no-limit hold 'em as well as I ever have—and that if I play with anything like the form I've achieved of late, I will surely finish in the money, and maybe at the final table.

"What about winning the damn thing?" he wonders.

I tell him, "Honestly, I haven't let myself think about that."

"Well, you better," he advises. "None of those guys play any better than you. None of them. You're putting them up on a pedestal. But I think you'll find the more you play with them, they don't know anything you don't. You can play with any of them."

I thank him for the pep talk. But the truth is, I don't really believe him. I've watched the Hellmuths and Chans and Ungars for years. I've studied them like lab rats, and I know—I truly know—that I can't think as they do. Some of the plays I've witnessed these guys make are utterly inscrutable to me, the work of maestros operating on a slightly evolved plane of poker reality that I can only hope to one day reach. Calling a guy down for all your chips with nothing but queen high? Folding kings before the flop when a volatile raise-every-other-pot maniac comes over the top of your raise? Moving all in with nothing but third pair? And being *right*. I don't get it. And that's why I know if I were to face one of these guys across the final table, with the title and the $1 million at stake, I'm certain I couldn't outplay them. I'd have to get lucky.

The vast sea of others, though? I'm not afraid of them. I relish the opportunity to match wits and skill and heart.

So many players, I've noted over the past year, seem to be very much like I was six years earlier: smart and accomplished and talented—but only about half as smart and accomplished and talented as they believe them- selves to be. It's not that they're arrogant or delusional.

They're merely mistaken. They make errors—errors they aren't even aware are errors—that I used to make and can now recognize. I'm not talking about monumental gaffes, just subtle little things (slightly overvaluing certain starting hands; overbetting certain pots; playing cards instead of people) that, when added together, separate the good players from the very good ones and the very good ones from the greats.

The vision I've acquired from playing in—and winning at—numerous no-limit tournaments has allowed me to better assess the quality of my opponents. And more important, it's allowed me to better assess myself. I feel as though, monk-like, I've attained a sense of wisdom about this game that I lacked several years ago—and that the vast majority of players, it seems, continue to lack. This vision, this knowing, instills in me a sense of calm, much like what I imagine deeply religious people feel when they have come to "know" their god.

Of course, I've always believed such zealots to be profoundly deluded. So perhaps I'm truly no better off than I was the year before, only more full of specious theories and ersatz power.

At the 1999 World Series of Poker, I arrive at the Horseshoe several days before the main event commences and promptly play, and lose, my first satellite. I play as well as I know I can, but get eliminated by an improbable and statistically rare series of so-called bad beats. I march over to the registration desk and buy in for $10,000 cash. It's my symbolic way of proclaiming that no amount of infortuitous river cards can keep me from my rightful place in the elite field of poker titans. And on a simpler level, I know—I mean I really *know*—I'm going to win more supers than I lose. The fields are just too weak, too mistake prone, too unwise. Sure, there are wild variances in the short term and the cream doesn't necessarily always rise above the curds. But my expected value, were I able to play super satellites every night of my life, is enormous. Given the quality of the fields, I feel as though I'm the casino, raking off my demonstrable edge hand after hand.

Less than 24 hours after purchasing a seat in the 1999 World Series of Poker World Championship, I win one (which I sell to a value-minded pro for $9,900 in cash) after a total investment of $620. And 24 hours after that I do it again for $220 and pocket nearly $10,000 in profit.

My success at the tables is doubly satisfying, since I've just published a collection of gambling stories, *The Man With the $100,000 Breasts,* and amid the book signings and media interviews and general good wishes from the stars of the poker community I've long written about, I'm actually *playing* like a member of that rare fraternity. No different from the theater critic who feels compelled to write Broadway musicals or the golf-equipment salesman who feels compelled to qualify for the U.S. Open, I'm infinitely happier being a participant than an observer —and not just a dilettante and dabbler, but a force. When Emile Zola was reporting the Dreyfus trial, so deeply did he immerse himself in the minutiae of the case that it was said he knew more about the affair than the judge and lawyers combined. My reportage of the gambling world hasn't probed even fractionally as deep as old Emile's, but I feel a similar sense of intimacy and expertise, if only from some sort of weird osmosis in which the collective brilliance of my essay subjects has somehow seeped through my pores. I no longer feel like a writer who plays poker, but a poker player who writes.

All seems right with the world. I'm playing beautifully, my book is a critical and commercial success, and I'm in love with a goddess of a woman, the magical T, who has made the past two years of my life happier than I could previously imagine.

I can't wait for the World Championship to begin.

On Day One I play the best poker of my life.

For eight hours I hold a legitimately powerful start-ing hand exactly twice, yet I manage to churn my $10,000 stake into nearly $26,000. My table is unusually weak for a major tournament—mostly satellite winners and a few low-limit grinders taking a once-in-a-lifetime shot—and I feel as though my opponents are playing with their cards turned up, a glorious state that makes the preposterously difficult game of poker seem ridiculously easy. So acute are my reads (my assessments of who has what) that I can play fiercely and cleverly despite holding virtually nothing of worth the entire day. The one time I have aces wired—ah, *that* hand again—I re-raise a not very good player, a reckless heavy-breathing fellow from Wiscon-sin, before the flop. With little consideration, he calls. When the flop comes down unmatched rags, I bet the size of the now rather juicy pot. The Cheesehead, reduced to a jumble of tells, huffs and puffs and fiddles his chips. I see his trembling fingers and quivering lip and I know my aces are no longer any good. He re-raises, as I al-ready knew he would, and after not much consternation, I toss my cards face-up into the muck.

The others at the table are wide-eyed and credulous. But I have no doubt—zero—that my previously unbeat-able starting hand has been run down from behind. And that's that.

Several of the railbirds chirp excitedly about what has just transpired—*"No, he didn't slow play 'em. He raised and the other guy called and then ..."*—and two of my tablemates merely nod affirmatively and say, "Tough decision." And I know everyone at this particular table at Binion's Horse-shoe knows for certain that, save for the most outrageous quirk of implausible fortune, there is no way in the world they can beat me at no-limit hold 'em.

Twenty minutes later I pick up kings on the button, get called by a desperate woman in the big blind, flop a set, play it slow and cool and controlled for every dollar it's worth, and reap the spoils of what's left of her stack when she makes an impotent two-pair on the end.

This is how it's supposed to work in a perfect universe.

When play concludes at the end of the first day, I'm in the top 40 in chips, poised to make a run for the money tomorrow—my first foray into Day Two—and supremely equanimous about the state of my game and the state of my life.

At this moment I like poker very much.

Hubris, as Aeschylus and Sophocles and scores of ancient sages have taught us, is … well, a tragic flaw. And while it may produce a sense of catharsis in the rest of the World of Series of Poker field—not to mention the attentive reader—in me it produces only a sense of profound disgust.

Hubris is what knocks me out of the 1999 World Championship on Day Two. Not obnoxiousness, not arrogance, not cockiness, not braggadocio, not delusions of grandeur. (All of which I'm eminently capable of periodically exhibiting, just not now.) What knocks me out is pride—pride in abilities that have ripened like so many juicy Cabernet Sauvignon grapes on a vine, but failed to mature and soften like so many bottles of young Bordeaux in a cellar.

For five hours I play unspectacular poker against a table of players who are approximately ten times tougher than the previous day's ensemble. (On the second day seats are re-drawn at random.) This group of no-limit experts plays a classical game: circumspect, aggressive, and unpredictable. They are much harder to read and much harder to take advantage of. Moreover, the player with the table's largest trove of chips, a wily Persian fellow who languidly chain-smokes Camels, is sitting directly to my left, ready to punish me if I step out of line too brashly or boldly. Without holding good cards, I find it monstrously difficult to make gains against these fierce competitors.

Lacking what a poker buddy of mine calls "psychological ascendancy" over the table (which, in layman's terms, means "everyone's scared of you"), I can do little more than tread tournament water, picking up some small pots a few times an hour and folding just about everything else. Now, if the blinds and antes didn't escalate every two hours, this would be a fine way to survive infinitely. But faced with progressively bigger stakes at each new level, contestants must consistently grow their war chest or face annihilation by those who have. At the start of the day I had one of the bigger stacks at my table. Five hours later I'm well below average—and I've barely lost a dollar!

Near the beginning of the day's third level of play, our table is "broken" (players are re-assigned to other tables who have lost contestants) and I'm moved across the room to one of the worst spots in the tournament. I'm sandwiched between Erik Seidel, a former New Yorker I've written about admiringly who has finished as high as second in this event and won many others, and a fast-playing Vietnamese dude whose style I find impossible to read.

To the observant player with a slightly below-average stash of chips, getting transferred qualifies as something of a bad break. The hours of mental notes you've taken on the eight other opponents at your table are instantly useless, and any judgments you make about the new octet you face must be made from past experience or intuition, neither of which are typically as effective as observation and deduction. Part science, part art, reading people is the rare skill that makes no-limit poker such a thrill to play. And without it—no matter how well-versed you are in probabilities—you can't win.

My drought of useless starting hands continues to vex me. I'm forced to periodically glance down at my two cards, not really look at what I'm holding, pretend I've seen a big pair—and then play my hand as though it's the real thing. Usually the other guys fold. But when someone plays back at me, I have to look carefully to see what I have and reconsider my options.

Stuck between a potential World Champion on my left—Seidel will, in fact, go on to finish sixth in 1999—and a potential chip inhaler on my right, I've got nothing going for me at the moment but my people skills. They're what got me to this position, I remind myself, and they're what will see me through to the next level, when, I hope, I'll get hit by the deck and find brilliantly colored stacks of red-white-and-blue $1,000 chips flung my way.

Did I mention this hubris concept?

For nearly an hour I've been watching everyone at my table like I'm a leopard lying in wait, camouflaged and patient, but ready to spring when the injured or feeble cross my deadly path. I've noticed a rotund bespectacled man with a short shock of peppery hair playing just a few more pots than he statistically ought to be. He's taking advantage of my—and most of the other players'—tendency not to make expensive pre-flop raises unless there's something that warrants such a display of power. He's been sneaking in out of position to see flops for a cheap price, trying to make something, and quickly exiting if he doesn't connect. But I've noticed that when this round fellow in seat four gets raised or in any way put to a tough decision, he predictably mucks his hand. I can almost hear him thinking out loud: *I didn't have much to begin with anyway, so there's no use getting involved against better hands unless I flop a monster.*

I generally like seat four's strategy. But those of us who pay close attention to his play—I assume Seidel and the Vietnamese assassin have noted this pattern as well—will take advantage of him in one of two ways. Either we'll push him off hands with nothing, or we'll let him play along with his slightly inferior starting cards, let him make just enough of a hand on the flop to feel he's got a winner, then charge him full price for a peek at the best hand. At least that's what I *plan* to do. The problem is, by the time the action gets around to me in seat nine, one or more hungry jackals has already gotten his teeth into the prey, and I'm forced to watch. (And dribble off more chips to the inexorable blinds.)

My stack has been depleted to less than $20,000 now, and I know I truly must start playing, no matter how marginal my starting cards, or whatever leverage and threat I once possessed will be rendered useless.

Finally, something good happens. My round pal in seat four looks over his glasses and blithely tosses in a call from early position. One off the button, I look down and find the ace-king of hearts. I raise three times the size of the blind. Everyone folds except, as I suspected, seat four.

The flop contains three small rags of three different suits. Player four checks to me. I bet the size of the pot, fairly certain that, having noticed I haven't played a hand since I sat down at his table, my opponent will credit me for a big holding and go quietly into that good night.

Instead, he calls.

Hmm. Curious. I look my man over. I apply my, um, world-class reading skills to him—hello, hubris!—and determine beyond a doubt that he is prospecting. One more unhelpful card and he'll be gone.

The dealer turns another small card, pairing the board and creating a flush draw. Now the board reads 7♣ 4♠ 2♦ 4♣.

Seat four checks. Thanks to all sorts of extraordinarily esoteric reasons that I can no longer recall and wouldn't be able to elucidate even if I could, I now know he has something like A-10 or A-J and I've got him drawing dead to two or three cards.

I bet the pot, about $6,000 now.

He immediately looks down at his chips—uh oh, bad sign—fiddles with his cards, and rests his chin in his palm. I can see (and hear) him breathing. The man is either putting on a tremendous act or he's beaten like a dirty rug and doesn't want to acknowledge it. Now, I would like very much for him to come to this realization. After all, I'm holding merely an ace high, albeit the best possible ace high. I would dearly love to add these chips to my stack and get back in the battle. I would like to reassert my—

He calls.

Hmm. Curious. When faced with heat, my man is supposed to crumble meekly. I mean, that's what I saw; that's what I read. Very curious, indeed.

As the dealer puts out the river, I watch seat four, not the card. After staring at the middle of the table for a few seconds, he looks up and catches me eyeing him. He looks back at the flop, looks at me, and says, "All in."

Seat four pushes his last $9,000 into the pot.

I look to the cards to see what has inspired this momentary bout of madness. There, on the end of the flop, is the king of clubs.

Since I know without question that a player who has survived this long in the greatest poker tournament in the world—there are only about 125 players left—would never commit so many chips on the flop and fourth street to a backdoor flush draw, I can eliminate the possibility that seat four has a flush. And thanks to all sorts of other incredibly complex calculations that I can no longer recall or smartly express, I can confidently eliminate a whole bunch of other winning hands he could possibly be holding. Which leaves only a lot of second-best hands or an outright bluff.

But beside all that exquisite analysis and logic and science, I have something artful going for me: my impeccable reading skills. I don't have to fret over the practical exigencies of card sequences; I can rely instead on the ephemeral alchemy of people reading. Magic triumphing over intellect, and all that.

I look at seat four. I see. I see his hands and his eyes and his neck and his chest and his posture and his lips.

I see into his soul.

And I know those chips he has foolishly committed to the pot in a piteous attempt at a bluff are now mine.

I'm Johnny Chan. I'm Stu Ungar. I'm a wizard who doesn't need the nuts to call a guy down for all the money. I have reached a higher plane.

Smiling—yes, actually smiling—I say, "I call," and flip up my ace-king.

"Flush!" seat four yelps, revealing his queen-nine of clubs.

It will be another year, approximately, before I will know what it feels like to have everything you believe in be exposed as a pernicious lie, but when it does happen—and it will, I assure you—I will look back on this moment and remember that, yes, I once felt this way, gasping for air, grasping for solace.

To be so right and so very wrong.

Ten minutes later I put in my last $1,800 with a pair of tens, get called by a pair of jacks, and say goodbye to the 1999 World Series of Poker.

As I speed-walk out of the room toward the elevators, I hear Bob Thompson, the Horseshoe's new Tournament Director, announce on the intercom, "We just lost Michael Konik, author of *The Man With the $100,000 Breasts.* Just knocked out on table forty-one."

Fighting back tears, like a weepy sentimentalist watching a sweet love story on an airplane, I resolve to reread Sophocles before I play another no-limit poker tournament.

Many successful men like to remind the chroniclers of their fabulous ascent to the pinnacle of their professions that the monumental triumphs they have enjoyed, whether on the golf course or Wall Street or in the research lab, couldn't have been accomplished without the support of a remarkable woman. I myself have been told this in so many words by Jack Nicklaus and Raymond Floyd, Jerry Rice and Dick "Night Train" Lane, T.J. Cloutier and Scotty Nguyen, not to mention nearly a half-dozen other luminaries accustomed to having the spotlight shining on their every exploit. Some of these men recite this sentiment, I think, out of guilt, remorseful for not having been better husbands and fathers in their single-minded quests to be the best at whatever occupations captivated their souls. Others say it because it's the most expedient way to utter the words "I love and adore my wife" without actually uttering those exact words.

But I think there's some inherent truth to the idea; I think that all of us do better on our individual stages with a strong and loving partner waiting in the wings. (I know I do.) I have found that I play my best poker, my most liberated and unfettered poker, when my home life is sweet. Strong. A terrifically contented feeling washes over me when I'm playing a poker tournament and, amid the pressures of constant decision-making, I remember that no matter how I perform, whether I win or lose, a sublime woman will be waiting in our bed for my return—and she'll feel as she does about me whether I play well or badly. It's a quick and effective way of putting the vagaries of gambling into perspective: The money and the championship titles and all the rest really mean very little when measured against the love of a good woman.

At the 2000 World Series of Poker, for the first time in many years, I am playing in a major poker tournament without an emotional anchor. I am alone.

This sorry state of solitude wouldn't feel so bad if not for … well, if not for one disappointment after another accreting like so much rust on the valves of my heart.

For several months I contemplated skipping the tournament altogether, reasoning that my flummoxed emotional state wouldn't allow me to play well enough to make my entry into the Main Event a positive expectation. It wasn't that I thought I wouldn't be able to concentrate well enough to make good decisions; my concern was that when faced with the inevitable misfortunes that are an intrinsic part of the game, I would crumble—so fragile and battered did I feel. I mean, it takes strength and equanimity to have the best hand run down by a 22-1 underdog. It takes clarity and vision to see such calamities for what they really are and what they really mean—short-term variances in a long continuum of results—and not assign to them all sorts of spurious symbolism that accomplishes little and breeds self-pity. And I wasn't sure I had the strength, the emotional resilience, to absorb and deflect the psychological pummeling that inevitably accompanies a four-day poker tournament.

But the counter-argument, helpfully proposed by my non-gambling therapist, was that continuing with my life "normally," doing all the things that typically give me joy, would be an affirmative statement of wellness, a proclamation to myself—and certain unseen others—that no matter what injuries of the heart I had suffered, I was still whole enough to carry on. Paradise lost but then regained—something Miltonian like that.

Still, with only a few days left before departing Los Angeles for Las Vegas, I'm not convinced I want to play. I am, however, absolutely convinced that I don't want to repeat *ad infinitum* my relationship travails of the past year to dozens of people I hardly know but see frequently on the tournament trail. So, instead of arriving four or five days before the Main Event per my usual schedule, I plan to arrive two nights before, leaving time to play a super satellite or two, as well as the dreaded (and unwinnable) Horseshoe free-roll press tournament.

On the morning of the Friday I'm to depart, I harvest a large bouquet of herbs and flowers from my backyard garden. I'm meeting N for what promises to be a supremely romantic date. If all goes well—and I can just tell it will—I may not be alone during the 2000 World Series of Poker after all. N is an important member of the Las Vegas media, with whom I have had professional relations that always crackled with an undercurrent of attraction and flirtation. Following a series of deliciously seductive e-mails and telephone calls, we agree to rendezvous for a proper date at a superb French restaurant overlooking one of the Strip's premier ersatz lakes. I'm dizzy with anticipation, already calculating how we're going to maintain our neighboring state-to-state relationship.

The plan is for me to dash directly from the McCarran baggage claim to my table with N, whose deep eyes and full lips and saucy sense of humor are already making my knees weak from 280 miles across the Mojave. So I'm dressed in one of my best suits, clean-shaven and grasping the garland of lavender and roses I've extracted from my garden, when I check my messages one last time before departing for a week of romance, love-making, debauchery, giddiness, mutual discovery, high hopes, and, incidentally, the World Series of Poker.

There's a missive from N! Seems, let's see, there's something she wants me to know ... feels a little awkward about saying so ... isn't sure exactly how much to tell ... but wanted me to know in the spirit of candor ...

N tells me she has a boyfriend.

I swallow hard and instantly feel very bad about what I've done to my garden.

Standing at the World Series of Poker registration desk, watching the nice lady recount the $10,000 in cash I've just handed her, I feel overdressed. My light Italian suit—the one that fits me so well; the one that was meant to draw N's attention to my broad shoulders and slim waist; that one—suddenly feels like a comical affectation. The scent of rosemary and lemon verbena on my fingers suddenly seems effete. The fantasy I had of champagne and kisses with N suddenly seems as absurd as the one this roomful of hopeful but ill-equipped gamblers collectively has of winning the World Championship of poker.

I should be in T-shirt and jeans, stinking of smoke and whiskey, getting my fingernails dirty from scraping in chips across the green baize. Instead I'm an innocent boy done up in his best, left at the altar of romance by a girl he really liked, the one who was going to make all that transpired before seem like a faint memory. Woe is me. Boo-hoo. And so forth.

Rather than do the responsible thing and reconsider how I feel about playing in the World Series, I lower my head and plow on, undeterred. My maladjusted, maniacal response to the N debacle was to bolt from the McCarran baggage claim, speed past the luxe casino where we were to have gazed longingly across a crisp white tablecloth and flickering candles, and head directly to the grungy charms of Binion's Horseshoe Hotel and Casino, in downtown Las Vegas. And buy into the 2000 World Series of Poker. Broken heart be damned!

I told myself this was a fine and healthy way to remind my fractured ego that I'm all right. Indeed, I told myself even more forcefully, it's a fine and healthy way to move on, to do something you like and you're good at, to prosper. I told myself all this. But now, as I watch the lady counting my money, I'm not sure if that stack of hundreds represents a position of strength or a monumental bluff.

I probably wouldn't feel as badly as I do about the last-minute N revelation were it not for what happened with J. J was the magic elixir, the delicious nepenthe I would drink in with all my senses. And all my sadness would go away.

For many months previous to J, I met a bountiful series of interesting and smart and provocative and vivacious women. I liked many of them immensely. I enjoyed being with them, in and out of bed. But none of these splendid women ever inspired in me dreams of permanence, of lasting and transcendent partnership. None of them, I knew, would be my mate.

J was different. After but one date, during which we had a spirited discussion on the merits (or lack thereof) of *Madama Butterfly's* libretto, I was smitten. Drinking in her raven hair and golden eyes, her I'm-thinking-something-naughty smile, her thrilling laughter—for the first time in a long time I could envision spending my life with someone. J was perfect for me in so many ways: an *uber-fraulien* with the mind of a novelist and the body of an aerobics instructor. She was smart and confident and articulate; she was sexy and elegant and stylish; she was passionate and sensitive and imaginative. She was dreamy.

She was too good to be true.

171

Like Goethe's suffering young Werther—but with significantly less lyricism—shortly after declaring my amorous devotion to this extraordinary woman, I learned my affection would be wholly unrequited. I told J how magnificent I believed her to be. She told me if I really knew her—truly and fully—I wouldn't love her. Indeed, she promised, I probably wouldn't even like her. J had habits and proclivities that, should I know them, would either make me "puke blood or take out a restraining order" against her, as she evocatively put it.

As a younger lad, filled with evangelical Mr. Fixit zeal, I would have hushed my beloved and promised that everything would be all right. And even though it wouldn't be, of course, I would have tried mightily to change what I could not, in direct defiance of Alcoholics Anonymous and various other get-well organizations. Older—and infinitesimally, microscopically—wiser, I took J at her word. I was besotted, but not crazy.

Losing J—or, more precisely choosing to believe her—was doubly crushing. In the here and now I could no longer, with this preposterously beautiful woman, have trenchant conversations on, alternately, the banality of Monet's paintings and the piquancy of Pauline Reage's pornography. I could no longer marvel at her acrobatic mind and lust after her shapely bottom. I couldn't have her. What J's evaporation meant in the long-term, though, was even more troubling: Meeting a perfect woman, I had to admit, was impossible, an elaborate fiction I wished fervently to believe but, under sober examination, remained little more than a juvenile delusion.

That's not the kind of realization that puts you in jolly spirits. Or makes you want to play poker. Or do much beside lay in bed, your concerned dog staring at you quizzically, and listen to torchy Frank Sinatra records about the one that got away.

I should explain. There's some history—some "backstory" as my colleagues in the screenwriting trade like to say. See, what happened with J—and with N, and with everything else in my life leading up to the 2000 World Series of Poker—probably wouldn't have felt so bad, or even felt like it mattered at all, if not for T.

T was my lover for three years. She was there when I played in my first World Series of Poker Main Event. She was there when I won and she was there when I lost, especially when I lost, ready to console me with kind words and a warm embrace and a perspective-illuminating kiss. She was my best friend.

Among her many charms, including her abundant physical attributes, I discovered what most appealed to me about T was her ability to teach me. Thanks to a bookish childhood and an even more bookish adulthood, I know lots of facts, mostly useless stuff that comes in handy on game shows, but doesn't necessarily help one live a life. I'm pretty well-educated, I think, but not very wise.

T taught me wisdom. Though she has the irresistible figure of a centerfold, and mischievous blue eyes, and a magnificent mane of auburn hair, and deliciously fair and freckled Irish skin, T is no mere sexpot. I mean, she *is* a sexpot. She oozes sex, and I've never met another woman more inherently libidinous, insatiable, and utterly unashamed of her libertine desires. But T is not a bimbo. She's clever, with an appetite for enlightenment matched only by her appetite for pleasure. When we met, in her native country of Canada where she held an important public relations position for a large hotel concern, I was instantly attracted to her alluring visage. When I grew to know her well, I was enduringly attracted to her mind and spirit. She was, to my shuttered eyes, a goddess.

173

T taught me many lessons, some of which involved her various interests in homeopathy, numerology, witchcraft, cosmology, and erotica. But the greatest and most profound lesson she imparted was this: Always be honest, no matter how difficult.

That sounds absurdly simple, a hackneyed homily imparted from the pulpit of a parish church. The power of this message, however, transcends the whiff of cliché that trails behind it. Before T touched my life, I was never able to master its simple premise.

I conducted many of my love affairs dishonestly. I ruined my marriage, a sublime storybook partnership to a woman I didn't deserve, thanks to dishonesty. Indeed, dishonesty nearly ruined my love affair with T.

But was I ever a great poker player.

Many have pontificated on the similarities between life and poker. And any sentient person can see those parallels easily: taking risks; weighing rewards; alternately suffering and basking in the vicissitudes of luck. Sure. Yes. Of course. But there's one dramatic fissure where the metaphor crumbles. In poker you have to lie to win; in life telling lies will only make you lose.

We all perhaps suspect this last bit to be true. And some of us may even believe it in our souls. But many of us—me included—confronted with enormous caches of evidence to the contrary, blasphemously suppose otherwise. We see liars and cheats and criminals reaping the apparent fruits of an American dream; we see badness rewarded and goodness scorned; we see righteousness trod upon in our civic offices and the halls of academia and perhaps even on our own playing fields and in our own living rooms. And we start to imagine that telling lies isn't such a bad thing after all. It's merely how one gets through life. We learn that one gets what one wants by telling lies.

T taught me otherwise. We had what most people

would consider a wild and untraditional relationship, filled with sexual adventures involving other men and women. (T is ravenously bisexual. I'm ravenously hetero. Our desires dovetailed nicely.) But the keystone around which our "alternative" lifestyle was built was candor. She showed me that the only way a man and a woman— a highly sexualized man and woman—could cultivate a lasting partnership was by fertilizing the seeds of passion with honesty. Unqualified honesty. No matter how troublesome, no matter how expedient the alternative, Be True! was the way, the only way, to be.

This, if you've ever tried it, is not an easy way to conduct your life. It can be painful. And tiresome. And way more complicated than anything not involving particle-string theory ought to be. It is, however, the surest method to construct a communion between two lonely souls that will last far beyond the pain and fatigue and complications of being alive.

This edict was not impressed upon me without considerable effort. I commenced my (initially "long-distance") relationship with T poorly, telling fibs—OK, lies—when that seemed easier than the alternative. The sexy neighbor across the street who sometimes brought me fruit after dinner? We were just friends, not one-time lovers. The charming woman meeting me in Vegas over the weekend? She was merely a friend of a friend, and we wouldn't be sharing a bed or any other intimacies.

My dissembling was, of course, found out, like an inveterate bluffer's continuous attempts to steal pots. And I was nearly knocked out of the game, if you will. But— forgive the strained simile—T allowed me a re-buy, a chance at redemption, where I could prove that my earlier misplays were not reflective of my real character and talent. At this stage of the relationship, I was made to understand that if I succumbed again to weakness, to the urge to tell the simple lie when it was more convenient than admitting the difficult truth, I'd be removed from the game as swiftly and surely as a flush beats a straight. T put it to me in a way she knew a poker player would understand: Basically, she told me, I must play our relationship face-up. Otherwise, she promised, I would have no shot at having her as my friend and lover and playmate, and every other glorious role we wish our life companion to play.

I couldn't bear to see T walk out of my life, so I resolved to learn my lessons well and, even more important, to apply them to every waking moment of my newly enlightened existence.

And I did. For nearly three years I told many lies at the poker tables, taking advantage of too-trusting opponents when I knew I could. But not once did I tell a lie to my beloved T. She was my inspiration, my mentor, and I vowed not to disappoint her. Or myself.

If you think I'm making too much of this accomplishment, consider how you would answer impossible questions from your earnest spouse. Consider how you would reply when asked to confront your deepest secrets, your blackest fears, your most private dreams.

Being honest is hard. But in every other arena besides the poker table, it's supposed to pay.

That's what I learned from T.

So it was with some dismay that I discovered in September 1999 that T had for six months been conducting a long-distance affair with some guy she met in a taxi line at McCarran Airport on her way to meet up with me at Caesars Palace. She'd been charmed, I subsequently discovered, by the fanciful story he told her of formerly being a gigolo based in Nebraska. On the pretext of doing public-relations work for his fledgling—and now extinct—T-shirt business, whose success hinged on the alleged humor in endlessly repeating a misspelled expletive, T met with the Cornhusker Gigolo several times on her out-of-town business trips, where he was invited to exercise the talents that putatively gained him entrée into the elite Nebraskan sex-for-pay industry.

To camouflage her illicit relationship, about which she (rightly) suspected I wouldn't be thrilled, T told me many lies. Not one. Not a few. A litany of them. And I believed every one.

Why wouldn't I? I was T's greatest student, a previously unenlightened dolt living by the pernicious get-away-with-what-you-can maxim that makes scoundrels of us all. But I learned. I learned so very well. My divine girlfriend showed me the true and righteous way, and I followed gladly, knowing I was blessed by newfound grace. All those others who took the easy way out of hard decisions would burn in a hellfire of their own making; I was headed to nirvana, with the flame-haired T leading me by the scrotum. Like the preacher who gets his congregants to sign over the deeds to their homes, she knew I had been utterly converted.

I was, in retrospect, a piteously easy mark—mostly because, like all deluded souls, I wanted so badly to have something to believe in.

Part of running a successful bluff is knowing against whom your lie will work. You don't try to get a guy to fold two-pair if he's the kind of player who thinks one pair is an unbeatable hand. It's been said—most recently by a friend of mine who is used to being cheated regularly by his business partners—that you can only be bluffed and betrayed by those you completely trust, for they're the only ones whom you'll allow to prance around your heart without cautionary guards. T knew her man. And she played me like a World Champion.

After learning of T's affair, I also discovered that she'd stolen from me large sums of money. She'd forged my signature on a check. She'd run up enormous charges on my credit cards. She had, for some time, been a consummate liar and an accomplished cheat. And I never knew.

I was all-in. My money and my heart and my soul were all piled in the center of the table. And I got bluffed.

The eight months between T's exit from my life and the 2000 World Series of Poker were not happy ones. Between therapy and grieving and longing and hurting, and trying vainly to heal the broken heart that I imagined was manifested with a large "SAD" sign pasted on my forehead, I didn't have much interest in anything. Particularly poker. Poker was the game where people got paid for telling lies. For some time this notion offended me. If you lied you were supposed to be punished. If you told the truth you were supposed to be rewarded. And poker had it all backwards.

This simplistic reduction of how poker (and life) works is, I think, indicative of how decayed my mind—not to mention my self-esteem, confidence, and sense of trust—had become thanks to T's hypocrisy. So shocked was I, so stunned, that I clung to the most rudimentary "truths" I could sink the tenterhooks of my mushy psyche into without collapsing in a bout of angst and despair. For a time I knew what the Catholic community must feel like approximately every other week or so when one of their beloved and trusted priests is found out to be diddling the altar boys.

Around six months after the T debacle, I began playing poker again.

And I went back to telling expedient fibs.

The most frequent one I circulated was that T and I had broken up because she'd decided that she wanted children more than bisexual affairs involving me and Las Vegas strippers—which was true, sort of, though far from the essential reason I was heartbroken. Still wounded and weak, I didn't want to relive my horror and disappointment every time someone asked me what happened to the shining goddess I had been living with.

I played mean poker during this dark period. I finished in the money a few times, but didn't win any tournaments. I was too impatient, too distracted, too *angry*. And eventually, I paid the price for being exceedingly aggressive and hostile. Observant players always noticed that I was an unhappy man trying to force results he once was able to conjure through magic, and they took advantage of my fury in the same way matadors defeat a charging bull. Like that noble but doomed beast, I ended up with a sword in what was left of my heart.

In one no-limit tournament at the Bicycle Club in Los Angeles, I was the chip leader at the final table. With seven players left, I should have patiently and masterfully carved up the remaining competitors, using the big stack of chips piled before me to jab and cajole and finally knock out anyone who dared to tangle with me. Instead, I called an all-in raise by the only other big stack in the tournament with something weak like A-J (so putrid was my call, I have forgotten the exact cards) and lost most of my winnings. I think I finished sixth. Why did I make this amateurish call? Not because of any well-reasoned analysis, I assure you. I did it because I wanted to change my state of mind right there; I wanted my life to feel better immediately. I wanted the pain to go away.

These are not good reasons to play poker. In fact, these can be very expensive reasons to play poker. Fortunately, I recognized my malady before impetuously deciding to pull up a seat at the $400-$800 game, buy in for $30,000 or so, and wreak a little mayhem upon myself. I resolved, instead, to take a poker hiatus until I felt a wee bit better. Because only then could I enjoy an evening of telling lies and getting paid.

At the start of every poker tournament, players engage in a curious ritual without overtly admitting to everyone else at the table that the ritual is occurring. Here's what appears to happen: Each competitor takes his seat, says hello or nods or counts his chips, then pretends to be fascinated by anything other than the octet of strangers ringed around him. But what's really happening is this: Each competitor silently and secretly assesses his opponents before play begins. Unless the talents of the combatants is obvious—*"Man, talk about a bad beat!"* a guy might exclaim, *"Three World Champions at my table and two of them on my blind!"*—the evaluation is done surreptitiously, with a sidelong glance, a quick peek, like at a single's bar where men and women play the charade of seduction.

At both the bar and the poker table, the participants know what the furtive glances mean, but almost no one admits these glances even exist. In the sexual milieu, this coyness, I suppose, is meant to be confident and flirtatious, particularly since the alternative—staring—is considered poor manners. In poker, the coyness is meant to conceal fear and weakness. If you make too big a deal of evaluating your opponents, the implication is you're terribly concerned about whom you'll be playing against. You should, naturally, have this concern. Your opponents are precisely what stands between you and the final-table prize pool. But most players like to behave as though the other eight seats are occupied by stuffed mannequins, that it makes no difference to them if the other contestants are World Champions or world-class chumps. Then again, most players, it must be said, don't look up from their cards long enough for the identities of their opponents to register, let alone affect the style of their play, which, it must also be said, is often mechanical and unimaginative. People who claim to have become proficient at no-limit hold 'em through computer tutorials often find the real world—where thinking, feeling, breathing human beings replace sophisticated software—a frightening place to play poker. And fear is not something a hunted animal cares ever to display—particularly when he has designs on being a predator.

This year I'm not sure whether I'm predator or prey.

And this year, without an affirming companion to calm me before the battle begins, I don't waste any time lying in my hotel bed doing breathing exercises or getting pep talks. Rather than wallow in my solitude, I mingle with the burgeoning crowd of players and fans, all eager to commence the 2000 Main Event. Forsaking the blithe, *oh-has-the-game already-started?* late arrival some cool cats favor, I encamp at my table early to do some pre-deal analysis.

My first impression is that I like very much where my table is located, in the center of the tournament room, near one of the room's two exits. (This makes quick getaways possible during the regularly scheduled breaks, as well as during unscheduled toilet dashes.) My second impression, as the table fills with players, is that I dislike the competitors who've been randomly drawn as my tablemates.

I'm sitting at what qualifies as a "tough" table. That I recognize (and respect) four of the eight other competitors is rare, especially given the record field of 512 entrants. The guys I'm most displeased to be seated with are Chris Bjorin, who has won multiple World Championships, including the 2000 World Series of Poker's big $3,000-buy-in no-limit hold 'em event two nights earlier, where he earned more than $334,000, and Todd Brunson, son of the legendary Doyle and himself a fierce player with an impressive resumé of tournament finishes, including second at the inaugural Main Event in Tunica, a new stop on the major tournament trail.

Bjorin, a portly Swede living in London who, I'm told, considers himself a part-time poker pro and full-time sports bettor, plays in some of the biggest live games in town and, from what I've witnessed, is utterly without fear. I've been seated at tables with him before and he seems to vaguely remember me (and that I can play some), though I'd be willing to bet he doesn't know my name. I'm in the #1 seat, directly to left of the dealer; he's in the #5 seat, squarely in the middle of the table. If we're to play classical positional poker, he and I shouldn't engage in too many confrontations, unless we both have big hands that require forceful investments, regardless of our spot in the betting rotation.

Young Todd Brunson, on the other hand, is sitting in the #8 seat. This means every time he's on "the button," in the favorable last-to-act position, I'll be in the big blind. Which, means, in essence, I can look forward to getting pounded most times I'm in the worst position. When you're in the big blind, you're compelled to put in a pre-determined ante bet before seeing your cards. (Thus, "blind." The metaphorical ramifications here are rich, but they're also obvious, so I'll let it go at that.) You are, in effect, committing money to a pot that your cards, once you get them, may not warrant playing. Sort of like throwing your heart into a relationship with a red-haired dream girl who may or may not be everything she seems to be. (Oops ...) Worse than having to invest money without foresight, the blind positions, directly to the left of the dealer button, have the disadvantage of acting first once play has commenced.

This may not seem like a big deal, but it is. Even if you don't gamble, you're probably familiar with the power associated with "getting in the last word." In a no-limit hold 'em game, the player on the button has the luxury of always getting in the last word—or, alternatively, the luxury of remaining mute after he's heard everyone else speak. Conversely, the big-blind player, two to the left of the dealer button, suffers the unenviable predicament of having to act either first or second—depending on if the small blind, who posts a similar ante bet that's half the size of the big blind, has decided to play his hand—for all subsequent betting rounds. So the key players in hold 'em tournaments are those who sit directly to your left and directly to your right.

When you're the button, you have the opportunity to bully the blinds. When you're in the blinds, you get bullied. Since the flavor of the game relies so heavily on position—at least when it's played competently, if not expertly—the players against whom you contend the majority of pots generally cluster around the button, and having a strong player acting last when you're blind means constant aggravation and pressure.

Todd Brunson is a strong player. What I mean by this is he's aggressive and fearless and, thanks to his pedigree and talent, has seen just about every poker play ever attempted, including some of his own creations, and he's not prone to be intimidated by some pensive writer-gambler with the unprotected blind money sitting before him. (Having played in poker tournaments with both Todd and Doyle, I can honestly say I'd rather play against Famous Dad than Precocious Scion.) Like his dad, who is huge, Todd Brunson is beginning to show signs that he'll eventually wind up a very big boy; every year when I see him at the World Series of Poker, he seems to have grown a few suit sizes—though a suit is about the last thing you would catch this kid wearing. He sports an awful mullet haircut, with the long straight back part reaching nearly to his waist, and a T-shirt-and-jeans ensemble that doesn't flatter his expanding physique.

Todd's heft, I should note, doesn't seem to prevent him from always having an overtly sexy girlfriend hanging off his shoulder. Cynics might claim Brunson's success in enrapturing comely lasses is another example of the intoxicating power of a large bankroll on the female libido. This may be true in many of the hilarious mismatches one sees in the gambling world—not to mention every other world—but I think in Todd's case the chicks actually like him for something other than his money and his biker-dude-meets-John-Daly coiffure. Todd is a genuinely sweet guy, with mischievously sleepy eyes, a perpetual grin playing at the corners of his mouth, and a pleasant sense of humor that seems to suggest he doesn't take anything too seriously, especially this silly gambling nonsense. He carries around an official-looking business card listing his occupation as "Investigator: Internal Revenue Service."

I know all this about Brunson because we spent one of the most surreal weeks of our lives together some years ago in Egypt, of all places, where he was ostensibly in search of high-stakes poker action against oil-enriched sheiks and I was ostensibly in search of a peculiar gambling story for my first book. When much of the promised action never materialized, Todd and I spent many goofy hours amusing ourselves in Cairo, where he taught me how to play a then-new and now-popular game called Chinese poker, which requires almost no poker skills at all. It was there in Egypt, beside the pool of the Mena House Oberoi Hotel across the road from the Pyramids at Giza, that I first learned from Todd the term "slow roll," as in when a player acts as though he has a losing hand, but then, excruciatingly, reveals that, in fact, he holds a winner. In a typical poker game, slow rolling is considered extraordinarily poor form, and its practitioner quickly earns a reputation as a lowlife. But in Cairo, where the professional gamblers in attendance had virtually no interest in the treasures of Cheops, amusement was in short supply. So Todd kept himself (and subsequently me) in a near constant state of giggles by playing low-limit Chinese poker and devilishly slow-rolling *every hand*. (In retrospect, I see that there's nothing inherently funny about this diversion, but, believe me, it was.) Thanks to shared laughs, a general proximity in age, and a mutual admiration for the topless Czech sunbathers on our Nile cruiseship, he was, for that week at least, my best pal.

Todd grew up around the biggest and best gamblers in the world, and virtually no occurrence in the poker world, I imagine, would startle or amuse him half as much as the bigger-than-life exploits he probably witnessed growing up in a most unusual Las Vegas household. There's not much I can do to bamboozle him.

For a few moments, sitting at the table sizing up my opponents, I catch myself hoping that Todd shows some mercy today at the World Championship, if only because he sort of likes me too. Of course, I quickly admit, this is an absurd notion, because once the cards begin to fly and the betting and raising and folding begin, best pals become the gambling equivalent of Serbs and Muslims. (At least that's usually the case. I've witnessed numerous occurrences of friends playing "soft" against each other. This doesn't necessarily violate the letter of poker rules, but it does contravene the spirit of the game, which encourages each individual to hunt down and slay every other competitor, including the ones with whom he just enjoyed dinner and cocktails.) If Todd punishes me too frequently and too well, I'll just have to see if he can take a joke. I'll unleash my secret weapon: I'll slow roll him.

As Todd relates a funny story about how he attempted to turn the label of the beer he was drinking at the final table in Tunica toward the ESPN television cameras so as to secure a sponsorship deal from the brewer, I evaluate the rest of the players at our table.

To my left, in seat #2, is a young chain-smoking Vietnamese lad dressed in designer everything. Generalizations based on race are insensitive and inappropriate, not to mention frequently wrong, I'm aware. So let me apologize in advance for being a horrible person. The Vietnamese tournament-poker contestants—*generally*—are remarkably good players. In my experience, the majority of Vietnamese poker pros take advantage of the Occidental misconception that all Orientals are degenerate gamblers dependent on inscrutable superstitions to guide their wagering decisions. The truth is, most of these guys, diminutive in stature and enormous in heart, play with a potent mix of discipline and aggression. A (white) poker-playing friend of mine who did three tours in Vietnam as a United States Marine morbidly jokes that the poker world would be a safer place if we would have won the war. That way, he says, "none of those little fuckers would have immigrated here on their boats and started winning all the poker tournaments."

Crudely as he puts it, my friend has a point. Look at the results from poker tournaments around America— particularly those in Nevada and California—and the frequency of Mas and Nguyens, Dangs and Phams at final tables will startle you. Fantastical as it sounds, some of these guys actually did come over on boats, with the proverbial $20 in their pockets and heads full of golden dreams. Men "the Master" Nguyen, the grand old man of the Vietnamese poker community, was, in fact, one of these fellows. Proving that the Horatio Alger myth still applies to modern American life, Men transformed himself from a traumatized, broke, and confused émigré into a wealthy property-owning member of the upper-middle class—not to mention a multiple World Champion of poker. He's a superb competitor, prone to entertaining verbal outbursts that tend to mask the computer-like analysis he constantly performs on his opponents. I like Men. Dressed in silk shirts, gold chains, and platform shoes that elevate him slightly above the five-foot plateau, he's a flashy vision of a foreigner-made-good, and his generosity with friends and fledgling poker players is legendary. (Once many years ago, when I was still a young journalist covering the World Series with neither the skill nor the bankroll to play in it, Men won a tournament and, unbidden, slipped $50 into my hand one evening with the imprecation to take my new bride out for a nice dinner.) To the dozens of Vietnamese players on the tournament circuit—and there seem to be more every year—Men, I gather, is something of a Godfather figure, the guru to go to when searching for advice or instruction or a loan.

He has led his flock well. The Vietnamese players, for the most part, play in the Master's wildly aggressive style, appearing to frequently "gamble it up" but, in fact, only doing so when they sense weakness in their opponents or—surprise!—hold a killer hand. I hate playing against them. They're just too damn good.

Unfortunately, for the next eight hours, I'll have the distinct displeasure of having one of the illustrious immigrants directly to my left. I don't know this kid's name—it probably features the consonant cluster n-h at some point—but I've played with him before, and he's no bargain. The best way to handle a threatening dude like the man in seat #2 is to play back at him hard. As in life, the most efficient method for dealing with a poker bully is to slap him back occasionally, for there's nothing a bully likes less than to be victimized by his victim. (Or, in the parlance of my semi-literate poker brethren, "It ain't no fun when the rabbit's got the gun.") To make this strategy work, you have to be willing to engage in bloody confrontations, and you have to handle them like going to the voting polls in Chicago: early and often. I was hoping to have a pleasant, nerve-settling, first few hours at the 2000 World Series of Poker. With the Viper from Vietnam on my left, I can forget about waiting for

187

the 12th round to start unleashing volleys of punches. I'll have to start sticking and moving from the opening bell.

The other tablemate that concerns me is a suave young Latin chulo named Carlos, who made an impressive final-table appearance several nights earlier at the pot-limit hold'em event. I've never played against him, but based on what little I saw when he was competing for the big money, I know he's the real deal. Carlos, who looks to be in his late 20s, is from Madrid, and like many Europeans, he has cultivated an affinity for poker games like pot- and no-limit, where leverage and psychology supercede number-crunching. Before play commences, I realize I have mixed feelings about Carlos. On the one hand, I instantly like him. He's polite and kind, with a warm smile and sympathetic eyes. On the other hand, I dislike him for having a beautiful girlfriend (wife?) whispering words of encouragement in and raining kisses upon his ears. His richness underscores my poverty. I'm displeased to have noted such a thing, even in passing. Before I paid my way into the 2000 Main Event, I vowed that I would put all thoughts of T and J and N and all the rest out of my mind and concentrate solely on playing world-class poker. Now, minutes before the first cards are pitched in the air, instead of focusing on future victory, I'm fixated on past loss.

Happily, Carlos' amore departs quickly, leaving me time to assess the four other less threatening players at my table. In seat #3, the guy who will be posting his big blind every time I'm on the button is a bearded fellow named David, who sports mirrored sunglasses and a T-shirt with the slogan "Competition is Fierce" emblazoned across the front. People whose clothes make epigrammatic proclamations, particularly quasi-combative ones, give me the giggles. I'm glad to have him as my blind boy.

188

Beside David, in seat #4, is a mustachioed man in his 40s who wears a windbreaker and a white golf visor, as if he's preparing for an afternoon tour of some Scottish links. Small and narrow-shouldered, this fellow looks like the perfect computer nerd. I notice, however, that though he seems introverted and circumspect, he keeps his head up, observantly taking in all the "data" around him.

In seat #6, to the left of Chris Bjorin, is the table's most dangerous player. That would be Ned, a former taxi-fleet owner from New York City who, when I lived in Manhattan, was one of the most sought-after participants in a weekly no-limit game held in an Upper West Side brownstone. He was always an honored guest, because he seems to play as though he has no conception of the fundamental concepts of no-limit hold 'em. I've always found players of this ilk extraordinarily difficult to beat, as evidenced by my dismal record in the annual Binion's Horseshoe press tournament where, in something like nine years, I've managed exactly one final-table appearance and numerous early exits. In the press tournament, half the field isn't really sure if three-of-a-kind beats two-pair, let alone what constitutes a legitimate starting hand, so it's nearly impossible to read anyone, or to run a successful bluff. Ned is not as poor a player as the typical media leech running around the Horseshoe with a notepad in one hand and free buffet tickets in the other, but his cluelessness makes him nearly as troublesome. I'd almost rather play against the Vietnamese Viper and Todd Brunson than Ned. Of course, I won't have much choice. Since Ned plays approximately two out of every three hands dealt to him, it's a statistical certainty we'll engage each other frequently.

To the left of Carlos and Todd, in seat #9, the man who will have the button when I have the small blind is a quiet Caucasian in his late 30s who, based on what I've seen the few times I've sat with him, has a playing style that mirrors his personality. The guy almost never speaks, and he slumps down in his chair, as if to attempt invisibility, like the proverbial ostrich burying his head in the sand. He's what's known as "tight-weak," meaning he doesn't participate much, and when he does it's typically one of a few predictable hands. If he makes a big hand he pushes it; if he doesn't he slinks quietly away. Seat #9 projects an air of apprehension—which is not exactly the kind of aroma you wish to be wafting in the nostrils of eight hungry jackals. I know if Chris or Carlos or Todd haven't raised the pot by the time it comes around to Mr. Invisible, I'll probably get to see a lot of flops cheaply from the small blind. And when seat #9 does occasionally wake up to find he's been dealt something juicy, he'll surely bet it with five-alarm bells and I'll gladly tiptoe out of his way.

Given this eclectic roster of competitors, my plan is to play super tight for the first level, folding everything speculative and playing only large premium hands. This is not a revolutionary strategy. Whether they say so out loud or not, at least half the field asserts they will follow this game plan at the commencement of the World Series of Poker. But probably one out of four players who intended on circumspection adheres to his pre-deal guidelines. Adrenaline and testosterone and other naturally occurring brain-altering chemicals tend to transform even the most patient monk into a raise-the-roof libertine. The action begins and suddenly a pair of sixes looks like kings. But this year I think I can exercise the discipline commensurate with such a "boring" style. And the reasons I think so are not great ones: I'm a little frightened. I'm a little intimidated. And I'm a lot distracted by thoughts and emotions that have nothing to do with poker.

I wonder if my opponents sense this. I wonder if they read me for the wrecked man I feel myself to be. I wonder if they're glad to have me at their table.

Holding a cordless microphone, tournament director Bob Thompson, wearing his usual ten-gallon hat and embroidered cowboy duds, which work wonderfully well for Las Vegas and slightly less so in London, instructs the dealers to "shuffle up and deal." With a crisp riffle of the plastic-coated cards, the clatter of plastic and clay chips, and the ritualistically uttered "blinds, please," the 2000 World Series of Poker Main Event begins. Instantly, nearly a year's worth of travails becomes irrelevant. All that matters is right here, at this little table, at this little casino, in the desert. Everything else goes away.

According to my fold-immediately strategy, the A-10 I'm dealt in early position is unplayable. So too are the late-position A-5 and the K-J suited on the button. I even fold a pair of sevens when another player makes a modest raise. Strangely, I don't feel even a tinge of doubt as I toss these hands into the muck. Instead, I feel a sense of relief. For a brief time at least, I can avoid getting involved in ugly confrontations; I can avoid telling lies; I can avoid having to wonder if I'm being told the truth.

For nearly an hour I fold and watch, fold and watch, fold and watch. The folding part isn't fun, but the watching part is. I'm noticing things, constructing hypotheses, conducting highly unscientific experiments. I'm making silent proclamations and seeing if the evidence bears them out. Brunson is playing fast; Bjorin is playing faster; Carlos has observantly pegged me as an easy victim for blind-stealing; no one understands Ned. Like a titillated voyeur, I'm actually having fun, though I'm not ostensibly "playing" at this point. That is, I'm not contending for any pots. But in a weird counterintuitive way, I am participating. My role is that of the submissive, content to let the dominants at my table dictate how the game will be played. The observant ones—and only the mildly brain-damaged could not notice that the guy in seat #1 hasn't played a hand in nearly 60 minutes—will ascribe to me certain traits and proclivities based on my passivity. And they will either take advantage of my "character" or be manipulated by it.

If this all sounds vaguely sexual, it's no accident. I think poker played at the highest levels has a distinctly—though sublimated—seductive flavor to it, in which the participants choose, consciously or otherwise, to pursue or be pursued, to direct or be directed, to be on top or bottom. The dramatic confrontations in this game frequently occur when the previously submissive-passive player decides to be a whip-toting leather-clad dominatrix and order the previously bossy table bully to bend over and drop his drawers. As in life, when these role reversals occur, they can be simultaneously troubling and thrilling. And as in life, the first player to understand what's really happening often enjoys the experience most fully.

Anyone who says poker is "just a game" and should not be assigned such fanciful meanings has not spent much time around world-class poker tournaments. Though it's mostly camouflaged or simmering beneath the visible surface, sex pulses here.

On the other hand, for all its "outlaw" resonances, redolent of the gun-slinging Old West and backroom hooch joints, the professional poker world *looks* like a strangely sexless place—or to be more precise, a strangely sexually sublimated place. In most forums where men congregate—and even with the recent addition every year of several more very good female players, the poker room is still a predominantly male bastion—the talk inevitably turns to the human male's favorite topic: females. Men love to talk about women. Whether on the golf course or at the gym or at the airport business lounge, the conversation eventually turns to women, particularly their breasts and behinds and their facility for performing fellatio. In the poker world, however, this idle chatter is oddly absent. Sports, investing, restaurants—this stuff comes trippingly off the tongues of poker players as smoothly as Ernie Els swings a fairway wood. But the usual (and expected) banter about women? Only the most obviously attractive cocktail waitress dressed in the most overtly revealing costumes seem to be able to elicit much more than a raised eyebrow from a table full of professional poker players.

The Freudian explanation for this is that all the men in the game, flinging their chips in and out, dominating and submitting, are symbolically trying to "fuck" each other, trying to use another's charms (in the form of money and chips) for personal pleasure. Whether through sweet romancing, gentle cajoling, or overt rape, someone—and often more than one—is trying to conquer a weaker and not necessarily cooperative partner. To speak openly, then, about matters sexual, even if they're ostensibly heterosexual desires, would be to draw attention to the homoerotic qualities that shroud this game. And what Cadillac-owning, Republican-voting, Liberal-mistrusting good ol' boy wants to do that?

The more obvious reason the poker milieu appears to be such a sexless place is that the average participant in this "sport" is grossly overweight or in some other way physically unattractive. I don't mean a few fat people inhabit the poker world, just as in any segment of American society. I mean a plurality of the participants are heavier than they ought to be. This, of course, is primarily the product of an entirely sedentary lifestyle, in which the most strenuous exercises one encounters are tossing the car keys to the valet guy and carrying a rack of chips to the cashier's cage. For hours at a time a tournament poker player sits on a cushioned chair trying *not* to raise his heart rate.

But this is not necessarily why so many poker players are fat. From what I've observed at chow lines across the country, the poker player's general inertia is exacerbated and augmented by a preternaturally acquisitive outlook on life. Just as gobbling up all the chips on the table is foremost in a poker player's mind, so too, it seems, is gobbling up seconds (not to mention thirds and fourths) at the all-you-can-gorge buffet. Many professional gamblers fancy themselves gourmands, with refined tastes in gastronomy and oenology gleaned from dozens of comped dinners to casino restaurants. But based on the conspicuous consumption of prodigious total calories inhaled at poker tournaments, I suspect portion control—or lack thereof—is the main criterion in determining a dining establishment's relative merits. One frequently hears gossip about weight-loss bets—for stakes as high as $1,000 per pound—discussed at the tables, and though there's much talk among top players about going on a diet, most poker players wear their prosperity around their waist, like chieftains of a primitive tribe. When someone in the poker world is really serious about dropping a hundred or two hundred pounds, like former World Champion Jack Keller, he gets his stomach stapled.

Given this propensity for sloth and gluttony (and the unattractive results these qualities produce), is it any wonder professional poker has failed to attract the financial interest of corporate America? For many years, as long as I've been involved in the game, the leading poker publications have been promising that major sponsorship of poker tournaments is imminent, that "any day now" a handful of visionary companies will see the heretofore murky business wisdom in subsidizing the prize pools at major poker competitions. Apparently, the hopeful thinking goes, some big company with way too much money in its marketing budget will come to the conclusion that giving cash to a bunch of physically unappealing, devious, chain-smoking *gamblers* will do wonders for their public image. Well, who would you rather have representing your company? A neatly dressed golfer with a winning smile and a solid work ethic who displays his lean physique and hard-earned talent on television every weekend? Or some lazy slob with dirty fingernails, a toothpick between his lips, and unwashed hair erupting from a worn baseball cap? To almost no one's surprise—except maybe the specialty publications whose *raison d'etre* is to lead breathless cheers for the gambling industry (and publish their advertisements)—professional poker remains for the most part sponsorless.

A few times a year, you can find television coverage of a major poker tournament, notably the World Series of Poker, on one of the ESPN networks. But these programs are highly edited and condensed, a *Reader's Digest* version of a Homeric odyssey. The truth is, even if the majority of the protagonists weren't unappealing, watching poker can be excruciatingly boring, particularly if you aren't a serious player. Even when the final table features garrulously entertaining performers (and they're as rare as royal flushes), the typical poker tournament offers spectators hours of tedium occasionally interrupted by brief moments of gripping drama. Unfortunately, poker is not a viewer-friendly activity.

For one thing, you can't see what the combatants are holding beneath their cupped protective hands. From a distance it looks like several corpulent degenerates staring blankly at each other. Without omnipresent television cameras to prime the corporate pump, I suspect most professional players can look forward to many more years of gambling with their own money, rather than, say, Slim-Fast's.

Of course, I could be wrong. Just as I was wrong about T. And just as I might have been wrong to program my 2000 World Series of Poker game to the "super-tight" setting.

So diligent have I been in the first 90 minutes about

proceeding cautiously that when I'm finally dealt some-thing playable—like the two black aces I pick up in late position—no one wants to gamble with me when I enter the pot. Aside from Ned, who notices little beside the ever-changing height of his chip stacks (which grow and deteriorate in predictable boom-and-bust cycles), all the other players have pegged my opening style and chosen smartly to avoid me on the rare occasion that I show strength.

The only antidote for this malady is to "change gears," as tournament players like to say. I need to drive a little more recklessly while my opponents still take me for a law-abiding citizen respectful of the posted speed limits.

In practical terms, this means playing more hands—even a couple of cards that have virtually zero intrinsic value—and acquiring chips that a weak hand surely doesn't deserve. The optimal players against whom to attempt such thievery are the best, most observant ones, the guys who have (correctly) surmised that I'm hesitant to crawl out of my shell with anything less than premium holdings. For my first victim I select Carlos, who's been stealing my big blind with a scheduled regularity that would make a train conductor proud—particularly one with a penchant for larceny.

I put in my big blind; everyone folds around to the Spaniard; he peeks at his cards and utters a nonchalant "raise" while stacking $250 in chips before him; every-one after him folds; I look at my cards, an 8-2 unsuited, and say "raise." I match his $250 and put another $500 beside it. Carlos looks at me, smirks subtly, and flicks his cards into the muck.

A few hands later, Todd Brunson raises in middle position. Again holding nothing, I re-raise him, indicat-ing I'm holding a big hand. He furls his brow, nods, and surrenders.

The Vietnamese Viper lets me see a flop for "free"

from the small blind. The board comes rags and I check. He bets. I raise him. He takes a long drag on his cigarette, blows the smoke over his shoulder while eyeing me suspiciously, and folds.

These are not monumental hands. But they win me back all the dead chips (and a few hundred more) I've donated for the most part of the first level, while I waited timidly, like an invalid boy watching the other kids play ball from my lonely bedroom window.

I can sense the better players at my table have caught on that I'm playing remarkably faster than twenty minutes earlier. They know I'm probably not holding aces or kings every time I raise a pot. Therefore, I now expect some retaliation, the non-verbal equivalent of: *Fine, you want to play? I'll play with you then. But don't expect me to be nice anymore.*

This is a fine state of affairs, actually. Now no one can really be certain where I'm at—primarily because I don't know myself. I haven't decided if I'm going to throw my playing transmission into overdrive or spool back down to fuel-conserving cruise control. All I do know is this: Being a voyeur is fun; being a participant, even if it means the occasional hurt feeling or bruised knee, is even more fun. Nearly two hours after the 2000 World Series of Poker World Championship commenced, I'm finally a contestant.

And just as one who doesn't fear a broken heart makes for a most liberated and passionate lover, one who doesn't fear losing his chips makes for a most fearsome poker player. Something I've known for years, but allowed myself to forget for approximately an hour and a half, suddenly dawns on me: The most important elements in winning a no-limit poker tournament are people, position, and, subordinately, cards. Play the people, play your position and, oh yeah, play the cards. The money will come. I'm no longer scared of losing it, I realize. Perhaps

I never was. It was the residual fear of being bamboozled, of being made a gullible fool, that momentarily paralyzed me.

Before I can construct further metaphors connecting what happened with T to my initial performance in the Main Event, I get involved in a big hand. (Note to aspiring philosopher-gamblers: Metaphor construction during poker games is generally a bad idea.) Everything goes away. There's no past or future. There is only the present. If poker has a salutary quality, it's this ability to encourage—no, to *force*—the game's participants to live in the moment, free of old wounds and anticipated travails, embracing the vaunted *carpe diem* ethos more often talked about than honored. Like Cartier-Bresson's photography, poker magically distills life into a "decisive moment." Maybe that's why I love the game.

I'm dealt a pair of threes on the button. Chris Bjorin limps in in early position; Ned, as usual, pays to see the flop; everyone else folds. I consider raising when the action comes to me, but I'm concerned Bjorin might play back at me (whether he has a premium hand or not), and I would then have to release the hand. Many novice no-limit hold 'em players overvalue small pairs before the flop. The fact is, most of their value is implied. Only a fool—and there are plenty, believe me—is willing to put in most of his chips pre-flop with a little pair, even if he's "certain" he's up against two over-cards—for example, A-J. But if you can get in cheap and turn a "set" (three-of-a-kind), these hands suddenly become delightfully worthwhile.

My friend Hal Kant, known as "Deadman" for his previous career as the Grateful Dead's lawyer, is one of the game's best players, as evidenced by numerous tournament victories and even more numerous in-the-money finishes. His theory, which I've seen him employ many times with great success, is that no-limit hold 'em tournaments are best won by making big unassailable hands that can crush unsuspecting opponents who may (or may not) have held marginally better starting hands. The Deadman likes to make straights and flushes and full houses—don't we all?—and tries not to overplay top pair with a big kicker, as many less-seasoned competitors often do. Thus, in Hal's way of thinking, small pairs that require little investment are almost always worth playing. You hit a flop and you're a snarling Gargantua baring your teeth; you don't and you're a retiring Candide tending your garden.

So I simply call, hoping to connect. The Viper calls from the small blind, and David, Mr. Competition is Fierce, checks from the big blind.

The dealer lays down the flop: 3, 4, 9 of various suits. Instantly, I become acutely aware of my body language, which, I fear, may appear too calm, too pleased. Rather than do something rank and telling, like shake my head in disgust—yes, some chumps still do such things, even at this level of competition—I put my focus where it should be, on the other players. I get no indication of anything from the Viper, who checks. From David I do, something that indicates more than the usual interest, but he checks as well. Bjorin, who has cultivated the lucrative skill of pouncing when he senses weakness, bets a little more than the pot, $300. Ned, beside him, frets over whatever it is he's holding, which could be literally anything, and folds his cards while uttering some sort of non sequitur that would take more time to decipher than it's worth. Now it's up to me.

I have two options: I can call Bjorin and hope for more callers behind me, in the form of the Viper or Mr. Fierce. Or I can raise.

After brief consideration, I raise—$1,000 more, to be exact, one little red-white-and-blue plastic disc. My hope is that Bjorin, who limped in early position with a big pair, likes the small flop and might get married to his presently beaten starting hand. Furthermore, he's the kind of highly evolved player who can win hands without holding anything, merely by applying pressure in a timely and accurately aimed fashion, like a jiu-jitsu master pinching a nerve in his opponent's neck. He might try to test my will and conviction with a re-raise; given the three-of-a-kind I now possess, it won't take much soul-searching to find the gumption to answer his inquiry.

Subordinately, there's something about the Fierce One's demeanor that tells me he's pleased with what he's holding. It's not a particular behavior or overt gesture that tips me, just a subconscious message that has somehow made it to my consciousness. Where this faculty was nine months earlier when T was offering herself on all fours to someone other than her True Beloved and systematically bluffing me into oblivion, I don't know. But at this moment at Binion's Horseshoe, my antennae are suddenly working.

The Viper folds immediately and lights another cigarette. Mr. Fierce looks at me and the pot and his cards, and then calls. I do not react outwardly, but I can feel my heart rate quicken. This little patch of green felt has been transformed into Agincourt and I into Henry V. Once more unto the breach, dear friends! A battle awaits.

Bjorin folds. He was, it seems, merely trying to steal this pot with an early-position show of strength. So now it's just me and the big blind. I count the pot. There's about $3,000 in it.

The dealer says, "Two players," and lays down the turn card, an eight. At this point, any card that doesn't complete an open-end straight draw—in this case, a deuce or a seven—is a "safe" card in my eyes. More important, I don't sense any change in Mr. Fierce's energy; I don't think the card changed his hand.

He checks. I consider being *très* clever and checking it back to him, hoping he'll try a big steal bet on the end. Instead, I opt for the better play: I bet approximately the size of the pot, $3,000. It's my biggest wager of the tournament and I can feel my breath shortening as I release the chips into action. Surely, Mr. Fierce will either fold or raise me here. For a variety of reasons that would be obvious to expert players and inscrutable to novices—and too tiresome to recount no matter your skill level—he can't possibly call my bet. If he were Chan or Hellmuth or someone similarly masterful, he could, particularly if he were planning on pushing me off the hand on the river. But he's not. He's a guy with a threatening T-shirt.

After thinking about ten seconds, he reaches for his chips. Immediately, I begin calculating why he is raising me and what my best decision will be. But before I can proceed down my logic flowchart, much to my surprise Mr. Fierce *calls* my $3,000 bet.

I watch him very carefully. Instead of torturing myself with running through an exhaustive list of *What Could He Have?*, I merely want to know the answer to one question: How much does he like his hand? The answer pleases me: He looks like he likes his hand, but fears I have a better one. How exactly I arrive at this information I cannot say. It's a combination of intuition and science, educated guessing and careful observation, Jungian behaviorism and voodoo. And experience. Sometimes you just know. And sometimes you don't.

But this time I do.

When the dealer turns the river card, an ace, and Mr. Fierce checks, I know my set of threes is going to win this pot. The only question is how much of a pot it will be.

My opponent has a little more than $5,000 left to play with, and that's what I bet.

I can almost hear him thinking, "Why didn't I fold on the flop? Why didn't I fold on the turn? Why did I have to be so stubborn? Now what?" And I'm pretty certain he won't be able to resist helplessly calling off what remains of his depleted chips.

I go into false-tell mode. Now that I'm certain I have the winning hand, I want to project an air of uncertainty and fear, not supreme satisfaction. The obvious way to do this—trying to look nervous—is not the most effective way. As Steven Seagal has proved countless times, bad acting always looks like bad acting. Instead, I maintain a look of blankness and stare at the chips in the pot. And I hold my breath.

Try looking completely comfortable for more than a few seconds while you hold your breath. No matter how relaxed you believe yourself to be, tension will eventually invade your features, imperceptibly at first, then more noticeably as the carbon dioxide fills your lungs. If Mr. Fierce bothers to look at me—and he'd have to be crazy not to—he would see a man who is trying, but failing, to look relaxed. And the longer this man, me, must wait for his opponent to make a decision, the more uncomfortable his visage will become, thanks to the wonders of lactic acid and other curious by-products of an anaerobic poker interlude.

When I was much younger I could hold my breath for nearly two minutes. (I spent many childhood summer afternoons at the Fox Point municipal pool, in suburban Milwaukee, Wisconsin, swimming underwater laps. Later in life I learned Frank Sinatra had endured similar self-inflicted torture to build his lung power, albeit in Hoboken, New Jersey. My breathless aquatic journeys had nothing to do with singing the Great American Songbook; it just seemed like a cool thing to do, slightly more so than performing cannonballs off the high diving board or peeing in the deep end.) Now in my thirties, two minutes without a gulp of oxygen would likely cause some sort of irreparable brain damage. While the

Fierce One plays with his chips, trying to imagine what life is going to be like without them stacked so prettily before him, I take in furtive little slurps of air, which, I assume, make me look even less functional, less right.

And of course, nothing is "right" with a man who is willing to mildly asphyxiate himself for the sake of a poker pot. But, brother, that extra $5,000 would do wonders for my early Main Event status.

Since Mr. Fierce has now taken close to three minutes to decide if he's going to call my all-in bet, I'm not in any way nervous that he has a better hand. If he did, he would have called immediately and with smug contentment. My "nervousness" now is the kind you feel when you're certain you're about to experience a first kiss. It's anticipation and wonder, not dread. Unfortunately, poker tournaments have too few of these delicious moments. Most of them more closely resemble standing on the edge of a 300-foot-high bungee-jumping platform while some annoyingly enthusiastic Australian guy with wraparound sunglasses and bleached blond hair stands behind you and loudly counts to three.

After a decisive shake of his bearded head, Mr. Fierce picks up his chips with both hands, puts them down with a pronounced thump, and says "I'm going to wait to play another hand."

He throws his cards in the muck and the dealer pushes me the pot.

I say nothing and show nothing, letting Fierce and the others wonder. At the World Series of Poker, seeds of doubt have a way of blossoming into weeds of insecurity. The less information I volunteer, the more my opponents must guess at my intentions. The greatest players at this game sometimes show their cards at the conclusion of an un-called pot. Their motives, I assume, are to condition and coerce the opposition into making mistakes. But I'm not one of those inscrutable masters. I'm just an emotionally fragile gambling writer operating on a decidedly terrestrial plane. I'll opt for good old reliable sensibleness over esoterica. No free clues.

The big pot brings my chip total to $15,300, by no means a spectacular total, but serenely comfortable. At the next level, $50 and $100 blinds, I can pay the tax for dozens of rounds, waiting for profitable hands, without feeling financially pressured to get involved in ill-advised confrontations. I'm already beginning to plan my tactics for the upcoming second level, which follows a fifteen-minute break, when I hear Bob Thompson announce, "Players and dealers, finish the hand you're on and hold up." Half the room dashes for the exits and the elevators. I, however, find that my ultimate hand at this level is one I want to play.

I'm two off the button holding a pair of sevens. Everyone has folded except for Ned, who, per his usual strategy, has smooth-called from under the gun. I raise several hundred, hoping Ned will get the message, get out of the way, and get to his room to enjoy the intermission.

Instead, he calls. The majority of our table leaves; they've seen plenty of poker hands over the past two hours. At this moment, the only thing most of the competitors at the World Series of Poker are looking forward to seeing is a waiting toilet bowl.

The dealer puts down a flop of little cards: 4, 4, 6. Ned checks; I bet the pot. He calls without hesitation, which is what he almost always does. Typically, he'll pay to see four cards and bail out when seeing the fifth one becomes too expensive. Still, I'd rather he would just fold and give me the smallish return on investment. Since I have trouble putting him on a hand, the less decisions involving Taxi Ned the better. Plus, I like the idea of ending the first level with 50% more chips than I began with.

The next card is an ace. Ned checks; I bet. Lots.

Against a typical player, I would bet the size of the

pot, a reasonably strong but not unreasonably dangerous amount. Ned, though, is stubborn. He doesn't do
things like calculate pot odds or play the player. He
merely looks down at his pile of chips, sees how many
he'll have left if he calls, and makes a decision based on
spatial relationships involving the relative heights of his
towers. The more I bet here—$3,200 to be exact—the bet-
ter chance I have of getting him to fold.

Besides, my sevens could very well be the best hand,
though I'm not clairvoyant enough to know.

To my dismay, Ned calls. My first suspicion is that he
has an ace and the turn card has given him top pair.
There's no other draw that I can see, except the absurdly
unlikely 5-7, which would give him eight shots at making a straight. He could also have virtually any unim-
proved pocket pair, some of which beat me, some of
which don't, and some of which he would have raised
with before the flop. I don't know. And that's not good.

I look him over. He seems happy. The ace, I'm guessing, made him chuckle.

The dealer flips over the river card, a jack. Ned moves
all in, about $9,000.

Clearly, I have to fold. This does not please me.

Though my decision is already made, I sit motionless
for half a minute, seething and staring. So much for the
vaunted "poker face": Ned is *smiling*.

A small crowd of contestants from other tables heading toward the exits pauses to watch the "drama," an
all-in bet being considered by another player. The truth
is, I'm not considering calling at all. I'm taking a few
moments to feel inordinately sorry for myself before re-
leasing my beaten hand.

After a minute or so of intense staring, in which I make
mental notes about what Ned looks like when he knows
he's holding a winner, I say, "I fold," and push my cards
to the dealer. Ned gleefully scoops in the pot, which con-

tains something like $4,400 of my money in it, and, un-bidden, shows me his A-K.

"What did you have?" he asks innocently.

"Pair of queens," I lie. "What did you think I had bet-ting all that money on the flop?"

"Wow. I guess I got lucky," Ned chirps.

I mumble something unintelligible that's supposed to pass for graceful sportsmanship and charge off to my room, where I know there's no one waiting to hear about how I've played, about how I feel, about anything. So much for keeping life's lessons in perspective. All I can think as I fume in the elevator up to my room is having $4,400 more at this moment would, I reckon, make me feel a bit better.

Either that or a lover.

Spend enough time in casinos and you will eventu-ally, if not rapidly, find people who are clearly bent on self-destruction. Their gambling habits, it seems, are some sort of perverse punishment for unseen transgressions and failures. No matter how much they claim to gamble "for entertainment" or "the fun distraction" or because they "always win," the truth is that almost all high-roll-ing (and big-losing) devotees of the slots and roulette and keno and baccarat and dice—and every other unbeatable casino game—play for dark psychological reasons that are probably better worked out for $100 an hour in the office of a caring therapist than for exponentially more in a heartless Las Vegas casino.

I've often regarded such monetary masochists with a mixture of pity and bemusement—but never with a sense of identification. I've always fancied myself too smart, too much of an insider with special knowledge of how the casinos bleed cash from their "unwitting" victims.

I've always thought I had too much, I don't know, character, to use a casino as a convenient way to expiate my inner demons.

During the tournament's first break, pacing in my cigarette-fragranced hotel room (the Horseshoe doesn't believe in modern amenities like smoke-free floors), I can feel the urge, the nefarious compulsion, to be reckless, to be self-destructive. To give it all away.

I suddenly understand why so many Las Vegas hotel rooms have windows that cannot be opened more than an inch. Though I'm not considering a flying leap onto the geodesic canopy above Fremont Street—which, come to think of it, would probably provide significantly more entertainment value than the nightly sound-and-light "spectacular" projected there above the heads of mildly perplexed tourists—I understand in my heart the not-very-healthy impulse to lash out at the slings and arrows of outrageous fortune with self-directed floggings.

Fearful I might return to the poker table and boldly push all my chips in on the first hand, I have one of those internal conversations that, were they verbal, would be utterly embarrassing. One of those, "Calm down. Everything is all right! Hang in there, champ!" kind of conversations that are best left to hackneyed action thrillers where the recovering alcoholic-cop-demolitions-expert single dad has to defuse a nuclear device enmeshed in the rafters of his daughter's grade-school gymnasium. I think the judicial system calls such skills "anger management," which wife beaters and bikers who delight in picking bar fights ostensibly lack, but well-educated writers are supposed to possess as readily as dictionaries and well-thumbed copies of Strunk & White.

So I return to the World Series of Poker World Championship event resolved not to be a destructive idiot. But now I know the awful truth: I have the capacity to be one. Maybe we all do.

Given the psychological contortions I experienced up on the fifteenth floor, the events on the second, where the tournament is conducted, seem comically banal. I was mentally prepared for Wagner; I get Gilbert and Sullivan. Thanks to one of those unforeseen collisions between poor cards and inopportune betting sequences, the second level, in which the blinds escalate to $50 and $100, brings me only two hands in which more than a few hundred dollars of my chips change owners.

On the first, I win $1,500 of ill-begotten profits from Carlos, who I notice is playing a bit faster than at the first level. I call his pre-flop raise with nothing but position. And when he bets the flop, as he seems to do on most hands he's involved in, I come over the top. He sighs disgustedly and folds. I feel like a *player*—and not just because I've run a successful bluff (anyone with chips can do that), but because, like a detective on the trail of a serial killer, I've read my man correctly and found a way to exploit his habits.

On the only other hand I commit to, my play is less commendable. Indeed, in retrospect, it's one of my worst hands. And one of the most instructive to me. Though I lose only $2,000, it is one of two hands that convince me I don't have what it takes—whatever that is—to win the World Series of Poker.

Unfortunately, it's too late to ask for a refund.

Playing from the button position against Mr. Fierce, I raise his big blind. He calls. On the flop he checks. I bet the pot. He thinks and thinks, and then he calls. (I have nothing; I'm almost certain he doesn't have anything either—maybe some sort of flush draw to complement the two clubs on board.) Fourth street brings a blank. He checks. I bet the pot—again with nothing but position. If he holds nothing but a flush draw, as I believe he does, he can't call here. (Well, he can't correctly call here.) But after losing so many chips to me on our big confrontation during the first level—*a hand he failed to call*—the Fierce One may be feeling a bit bullied; he may have surmised (somewhat correctly) that the writer dude in seat #1 has found in him a convenient target.

Now, if this is what Fierce truly believed, he would raise my sorry ass, slapping me back twice as hard as I've hit him.

Instead, he calls.

This perplexes me. Surely he couldn't be calling in hopes of hitting his flush. If a club comes he won't get a dollar out of me. He must know that. His call, therefore, is paying him even money on something like a 3-to-1 shot. (If you want to retire rich, offer your customers this kind of price; if you want to retire destitute, take this kind of price.) If a club doesn't come—well, he's got to assume he's beat and, as in the other scenario, also won't get another dollar from me.

In other words, he *can't* be calling a bet the size of the pot with one card to come holding only a flush draw. In thousands of casual games across America, yeah, sure, he could be. In friendly little $20-buy-in tournaments attended primarily by retirees and refugees from the slot machines, absolutely he could be. But not in the World Series of Poker he couldn't be.

So he must have something other than a flush draw— say, two-pair he's been cleverly slow playing while I mistakenly try to steal what's rightfully his. Ergo, since I am indeed holding nothing but a wee 4-5 of hearts and am probably beaten by Mr. Fierce's concealed strength, I cannot bet on the end. Q.E.D.

See how cleverly I figured that all out?

Here's a lesson my friend Pat, a seasoned tournament veteran, once taught me, which I'll graciously pass along to you without charge (though he extracted 10% of my winnings for a year to teach me this concept, among, admittedly, a few other juicy morsels of poker wisdom): Don't give the suckers too much credit.

This invaluable imperative took me several years to incorporate into my game. If everything about your opponent's behavior indicates he's holding a hand, no matter how unlikely it seems, he probably is, despite the apparent idiocy such a holding would seem to require. The correct question an expert poker player asks himself, I eventually discovered, isn't, "How the hell could he possibly have what he seems to be suggesting he has?" It's, rather, "How did I get so lucky as to be seated with someone who would play so ludicrously?"

In the case of Mr. Fierce, I wrongly gave the man credit for playing well enough not to call a pot-size bet with nothing but a flush draw. That was in violation of Pat's Law.

The final card is a blank. Fierce checks, probably with the intention of raising me when I try to bluff his two-pair. At this moment I know I can't win the pot no matter what I do—I have a five high!—so I check also, glad that I've only lost $2,000 on this clumsy hand.

To my amazement, Fierce turns over the Q-2 of clubs. "That wins," I say, trying to force an isn't-that-funny? smile on my stricken face. I've let the guy win a $4,000 pot with a queen high.

All I had to do, in blissful hindsight, was bet on the end. He would've folded, having missed the flush draw he thought worthy of such a large investment. The pot would have been mine. But more important than the chips, I would have proven to the table—and even moreso to myself—that I could win with or without cards, just like all the other champions who have earned the

Horseshoe's golden bracelet (and $1 million in cash.) Instead, I misread my man.

By not betting on the river, I proved, however inconclusively, that I wasn't ready to win this tournament.

I'd very much like to tell you that the previous passage was a terrific way to build dramatic tension, that, in fact, I *do* go on to win the tournament, despite my self-doubts, despite my tactical errors, despite my brief forays into self-pitying remembrances of the One Who Did Me Wrong. That would be a fairytale kind of story, wouldn't it? A fantasy. Something that could only come true in the fertile fields of a writer's imagination. A writer-dilettante, of all people, thinks he knows how to play poker as well as the best professionals in the world enters the 2000 World Series of Poker and somehow—how? how?—manages to beat 500 of the greatest card players on the planet. And lives to tell the tale.

Well, it happens. Sort of.

Just not to me.

Shortly after I buy in for the Main Event, on the evening of my arrival at Binion's, I run into my friend Andy, who has quickly (and deservedly) earned himself a reputation as one of poker's keenest observers. His sharply written accounts of major poker-tournament action, known in the industry as "wrap-ups," are the one readable respite in an otherwise unreadable journey through poker's leading magazine, which seems to pride itself in publishing people whose vast poker knowledge is inversely proportional to their command of written English. Andy, in his role as the "poker pundit," as he calls himself, keeps abreast of all the latest news and developments on the tournament trail. Tonight, he's got some news for me.

Seems the venerable *Harper's* magazine has sent a contributing editor here to the Horseshoe to compose one of the magazine's famously breezy and reflective essays on this grand and instructive event. The writer, I imagine, has been charged with explaining what it all really means, holding forth on what this tournament says about American culture, and, if I know *Harper's*, finding poetic but tenuous connections between the debasement of the American political system (particularly the Senate) and some poker game in the middle of the Mojave Desert.

Harper's is one of my two favorite magazines—the other being the *New Yorker*, which has published my friend Al Alvarez's seminal accounts of the World Series of Poker on two occasions. Though it lacks the *New Yorker's* ineffably wonderful cartoons, which single-handedly make life worth living, *Harper's* is one of the few mass-market publications still extant that cater to smart readers with smart writing. While nearly every other magazine in the United States—not to mention the galaxy—relies on the cult of celebrity and sex to move the merchandise (including the *New Yorker* in some issues), more than 150 years after two eponymous brothers started the enterprise, *Harper's* still trades in the far less reliable market of ideas. Though the magazine's current editor, Lewis Lapham, is sometimes too reflexively liberal for my libertarian tastes, his graceful "Notebook" essays, a monthly tutorial in how to be a great writer, set a lofty standard for the stories and arguments and investigations that follow. A mediocre writer occasionally slips through Lapham's editorial filter, but his magazine is consistently filled with good minds expressing themselves well. To me, one who finds so much of popular culture an embarrassment and an insult, *Harper's* is like a sanctuary, a literary hiding place where I can take refuge from our media's ongoing Apotheosis of Fame.

212

I've never written for *Harper's*. (Nor have I written for the *New Yorker*.) I have written *to* both those magazines and received some polite rejection notices.

Many years ago, when I was starting out as an author, I got some useful guidance from one of my first editors, an older fellow who, it seemed to me, knew how the words-for-hire business worked. This mentor of mine worked at the *Village Voice*, a Greenwich Village-based newspaper that, in the revolutionary spirit of the 1960s, could be reliably counted upon to denigrate "the establishment" and celebrate the works, however dubious, of the "alternative" community. And what was he doing there? Writing about tennis.

His advice was to find a subject, something that spoke to you, and become an expert on it, learning all you could about this passion of yours and writing everything you knew about it in whatever publication would have you. Eventually, he told me, when a magazine wanted a story on, say, tennis, it would know who to call.

When Andy tells me the *Harper's* news, I'm dismayed that they wanted a story about gambling and they didn't know who to call.

Though I've never met the man, I instantly dislike Jim McManus, the writer Lewis Lapham has assigned to cover the 2000 World Series of Poker. I'm sure McManus is a good writer—he's published in *Harper's*, after all— and a nice enough fellow, and maybe he even knows something about poker. But damn! He's got something I thought was mine. In this sense McManus isn't much different than the guy who was fucking my girlfriend while I looked the other way.

The one thing of his I have read—a magazine account of the McManus' incomprehensibly obnoxious insistence on inflicting their food-throwing infant daughter on the fine restaurants of Paris—had me convinced that the author must surely be one of the most ill-mannered asses to have ever visited France. Surely, only the most insensitive prick would subject fellow adults engaged in rapt conversation and silent seduction and sensual pleasure to the mood-killing antics of his screaming baby daughter. The guy must be an idiot.

Turns out after meeting him briefly that McManus is a decent enough fellow and a decent enough writer and—shit!—knows a little about poker. What begins in my heart as envy melts into admiration.

The admiration quickly devolves back into envy a few days later. Jim McManus, who is merely supposed to be here in Las Vegas to write a lovably literary account of the World Series of Poker, wins a $220 super satellite, enters the Main Event, and, miraculously, finishes fifth and earns more than $250,000.

Never mind that he frequently plays terribly along the way; never mind that his magazine account of his great luck is riddled with editing errors and inexplicable dullness; never mind. To my fractured ego and fragile psyche, what Jim McManus does strikes me as irrefutable evidence that, once more, I'm not good enough. Not good enough to write for *Harper's*. Not good enough to get in the money at the World Series of Poker. Not good enough to earn the faithful love of T. In retrospect, I'm able to see the general ickiness of this formulation. But at the time, while the cards are flying and the chips are clattering, the McManus revelation is more depressing than being all-in with a 7-2 offsuit against a pair of aces.

Several other professional scribes have played in the World Championship over the years, notably Alvarez, Tony Holden, and the late David Spanier, but none have ever finished in the money. I'd hoped to be the first of the ink-stained wretches to accomplish this unthinkable feat. Not only has McManus beaten me to the record, he's done it in a fashion—final table! on the Discovery Channel broadcast!—that can only be bettered by winning the thing.

And he's writing all about it for my favorite magazine. I guess they knew who to call.

At the end of the second level, I have $9,300, which is well below "par" (the amount of chips in action divided by the number of surviving players), but significantly more than Bjorin and Brunson, the two pre-tournament favorites at my table. They've failed to adjust their usual tactics to account for the inscrutable decision-making of Taxi Ned who, at present, has most of our table's chips. He'll give them back as surely as *Vanity Fair* will swoon over a handsome movie star's efforts to find a home for retired circus animals. But in the interim I can feel the other players' pain. (Having played with Ned for so many years in New York, I've built up something like an immunity; I've developed Ned antibodies.) Here's a guy who seems to get involved in every other hand and yet, in defiance of everything one reads in Sklansky and Malmuth and all the other leading poker theoreticians, somehow manages to gobble up the chips like a slot machine consumes coins. To expert players accustomed to competing against other experts, Ned's "strategy"— not to mention its apparent efficacy—must be maddening.

As I say, I don't mind it. And not just because I'm accustomed to it. The fact is, the more his inept poker abilities continue to confound the better players, the more apt they are to blow off their remaining chips. They know the correct way to attack an enigma such as Ned. (That would be: patiently, cautiously, imperiously.) But their emotions cloud their judgment. Having experienced this expensive syndrome about, oh, 496 times, I can speak with some authority about it. The cloudier a good player's judgment becomes, the more diluted his powers, and the less distinct the differences between his play and hapless Ned's. The Bjorin and Brunson I'm seeing are recognizable only in silhouette. I'm watching two captains who have lost command of their respective ships, as though they were two marionettes manipulated by a puppeteer who didn't know much about the game of Texas hold 'em. It's not really their fault. It's poker's.

Poker has a funny way of carrying your mind outside of your body, sort of in the way people who have come back from the dead describe their exit and re-entry from quotidian life. As in a bad dream, you see yourself from a small distance, close enough to observe every detail of your horrifyingly destructive actions, but too far away to prevent them. Someone else, it seems, is controlling your motor functions, your decision making. Someone else is convincing you it's good and proper and, in fact, utterly necessary to call off the last of your chips with an A-9 after two other players have raised and re-raised the pot. You know this is not really what you want to do. But when you're enraged and frustrated and perplexed, you can't help yourself. Rather than wake with a start and sigh with relief, you continue to sleepwalk through the game, oblivious to things like pot-odds and position and patience. Inebriated by the bitter wine of poker disappointment, you play like Ned on his worst day.

If you've never seen a losing poker player, I can tell you what he looks like: sad, bewildered, angry, resigned, inconsolable. Very much like someone mourning a lost love.

During the break, I retreat to my hotel room and look out the window at the hundreds of tourists wandering around Fremont Street, plastic buckets of nickels clutched to their chests like so many protective crosses. Standing in the doorway of Sassy Sally's—one of downtown's slots-only hustle joints—a tall young woman wearing a foam cowboy hat the size of a well-fed albacore tuna repeatedly drones "free spin, free spin" into a microphone. She's in showbiz now, I suppose. But back when she was growing up in, I don't know, Fresno or Sioux City or Staten Island, did she ever think this was how she would spend 40 hours a week of her life?

Seeing the girl in the hat encouraging credulous visitors to invest their social-security checks in her casino's parsimonious slot machines, I think back to my Wisconsin childhood. Did I ever imagine as a schoolboy that 20 years later I would be in a surreal city called Las Vegas, competing in the World Series of Poker? Playing with my neighborhood chums for dimes and quarters, I don't recall being aware that such a thing existed, or that I had any aspirations to participate in poker games—besides those in which the players stuck cards to their foreheads. Yet here I am, a man in his thirties, sitting in a lonely Glitter Gulch hotel room, exactly 12 minutes away from returning to the most important poker game on Earth, where the approximately 400 remaining players will test their skills against a roomful of people intent on sending them home with nothing but memories.

I figure I ought to call my mom.

She hates all this gambling stuff I'm involved in. To her it's slimy and distasteful and somehow unclean. My mother is a lifelong elementary-school teacher. She taught me to read at age three and filled my childhood with books and vaguely hippie-ish slogans, such as "Make Love, Not War," and probably secretly wished my brother and I would turn out to be Peace Corps volunteers. If she'd had her way, instead of writing about the underbelly of American culture, her elder son would be composing books about fine art and yoga and doing readings at nursing homes.

I love my mom very much. When something good happens in my life, she's the first person I want to tell, because the genuine happiness that bubbles out of her is often more fun and exciting than the good thing I've called to tell her about. My dad I love, too. He's more circumspect, a former Marine who feels and thinks deeply, but is less effusive about his emotions. My dad is a warm smile; my mom is hysterical jumping up and down and trembling hands. When they're gone, I'll miss them both. And nothing I accomplish in my life, I know, will ever feel quite as rich without being able to telephone them to share the news. Indeed, if I feel any compulsion in my life to succeed, to create, to win, it's because I want to do so while my parents are still around to enjoy the triumph with me.

This year I'm nearly certain I won't have any wonderful news from the World Series of Poker to share with them. And that's a shame, since they could both use a cheerful report from the gambling netherworld.

My parents' marriage of 37 years is crumbling. Nothing cataclysmic has happened—no affairs, no alcoholism, no financial irresponsibility. Their relationship, for reasons that are both apparent and mysterious to me and my younger brother, is not working. And for the first time in decades of partnership, they're living apart, lonely, frightened, and profoundly sad.

I sort of know how they feel.

Surveying the cluster of casinos below my hotel room, the liquid reflection of color across the way on the Golden Nugget's black-glass tower, I dial my mom in Milwaukee, knowing she'll be pleased to hear her son's voice, no matter how he's doing in that silly poker nonsense he's gotten himself involved in.

She sounds tired and defeated, my mom does, and I don't have the heart to tell her that this year, honestly and truly, I know I won't win the World Series of Poker.

Instead, I stress that I still have chips and that I'm thinking clearly. I leave out the part about missing T and occasionally being enveloped by a shroud of rage that
nearly makes me nauseous.

My mom tells me how poorly her counseling sessions
are proceeding with my dad. She tells me how sad she is.
And then, in the best uplifting mom spirit, she urges me
to get back to the tournament and play as well as I can.

I decide right then to do as she asks.

Professional golfers often talk about "grinding"—as
though their highly sponsored khakis-and-titanium live-
lihood involved spending the workday bent over a mill-
stone. In the parlance of the PGA Tour, a grinder is someone who scratches out his score one unspectacular shot
after another, hitting fairways and greens, making a few
putts, and scrambling imaginatively when his swing per-
forms unreliably. Grinders don't necessarily hit long par-
fives in two or execute stylish flop shots. They just go
about their resolutely unspectacular business, surreptitiously climbing the leader-board while the longer
flashier players make the highlight reels.

During level three at the World Series of Poker Main
Event, I'm a grinder.

Playing with $100 and $200 blinds, I grind my stack
back up to $14,700, $600 and $800 at a time. Never in-
volved in dramatic confrontations, never invested more
than $2,500 in a single pot, I bob and weave, stick and
move, picking up a few blinds and several tiny pots that
no one seems much interested in. Grinding is a fine (and
marginally fun) way to play no-limit hold 'em. You never
have to showdown your cards; you never put much of
your money at risk; and you steadily, almost invisibly,
increase your wealth and power.

Bjorin and Brunson both exit the tournament at this level, and the table's play grows briefly subdued, almost somnolent, as if observing a moment of silence for these two fallen warriors. With a couple of the "faster" contestants eliminated, the remaining players seem to enjoy a respite of equilibrium, when every move made doesn't have to withstand the rigorous inspection of the table's two leading heart-testers. With Chris off to a juicy side game and Todd surrounded by friends at the race-book bar, Carlos and the Viper nominate themselves for the now-vacant position of table bully. (Ned, with his mountain of chips growing like a high-school football player on steroids, could easily harass and manipulate anyone at the game, but he, inscrutably as always, prefers to make more cold calls than a boiler-room broker with a hot new penny stock.) Me? I grind.

A large gallery of onlookers, three-deep in some places, has formed at the rail. Some of the audience just wants to get a commemorative peek at what's touted as the world's best collection of poker players under one roof. For a first-time visitor to the World Series of Poker, I imagine the scene of hundreds of sullen people looking phenomenally bored must be a bit of a letdown. The gawkers come to Binion's with visions of outsized characters like Amarillo Slim and Puggy Pearson dancing in their heads; instead, for the most part, they get an eyeful of anonymous contestants, whose table comportment has about as much color as a Robert Motherwell painting.

Very large, very obviously armed security guards, dressed like a cross between highway patrolmen and waiters at a western steakhouse, deny access to the tournament arena to all but the contestants and accredited media; many of the latter aimlessly wander around the sea of tables, pausing momentarily to watch the action from a delightfully intimate perspective—like, right over some guy's shoulder—and scribble erudite memos (*Chan:*

playing well!) before moving on to their next free meal. Whenever an innocent scribe stays parked in one place too long—two hands seems to be the unspoken limit—he generally receives dirty looks from some paranoid gambler who imagines the fellow standing behind him with the notepad is actually a covert operative surreptitiously telegraphing his hole cards to the other players.

If you've ever seen the World Series of Poker Press Tournament, a free-roll extravaganza sponsored by Binion's, you know what a comically absurd concept this is. Most of the media in attendance couldn't tell you what the phrase "full house on the river" means, let alone comprehend the relative merits of various middle-position starting hands. (In fact, more than a few media contestants each year must show their cards to the dealer so they can be told what they're holding.)

Since so much money is at stake at the World Series—more than $5 million in the Main Event alone—correspondents from around the world come to the Horseshoe every spring in search of a good story, a compelling character, a cute sound bite. No one seems to mind that most of the tournament's interesting narratives have by now been endlessly repeated like a bad rumor, worn smooth by the hot winds of lazy punditry. In addition to the hardcore gambling publications, for which the World Series of Poker is like the Super Bowl to *Pro Football Weekly*, an astonishing variety of mainstream outlets descend on downtown Las Vegas to chronicle the mildly debauched mayhem. Even the curiously labeled "women's" magazines—how anything so baldly misogynistic as the average fashion rag could be considered a *women's* magazine is beyond my ken—show up every year to do error-prone stories on "women in poker." Invariably a fresh young news hound right out of Yale jets in from her New York City cubicle, endures the clumsy flirtations of the male players she interviews by the dozens, and hangs around with the insular Poker Girl Mafia just long enough to become convinced that these independent businesswomen would make terrific role models for all the office drones who read, say, *Cosmo*—never mind how socially maladjusted a singular focus on gambling tends to make people, male or female.

Then there are the small-market newspapers, which typically hope to document some hometown boy's Las Vegas dreams coming true. The fledgling reporter dispatched to chronicle the fantasy-in-progress, I've noticed, often disappears for 48 hours at a time and returns to his assignment with ashen complexion, a wicked hangover, and pockets that are otherwise empty, save for business cards from thriving corporations like Misty's International Escorts.

Most amusing are the members of the "electronic media." With the advent of the World Wide Web, almost anyone with a Web site can get press credentials to most any newsworthy event, including the World Series of Poker. At the press tournament this year, I sat at the same table as a British woman who worked for a porno site.

The throngs ringing the rails surrounding the poker action are probably more intently focused on the players than the television crews and digital-camera-toting Internet reporter-photographers, who transmit variations on the theme of facial blankness to computer users around the globe. Relatives and friends, investors and lovers all want to get close to their favorite player, though it's almost impossible to actually see what he or she is being dealt. Still, some "sweaters," as they're known, stand for hours at a time, religiously monitoring the ebb and flow of their favorite player's chip tide. They quietly observe his body language, his demeanor, searching for clues, just as his opponents are, of what he's really thinking and feeling behind the mask of inexpressiveness. Mostly, though, sweaters in the audience try to make eye

contact with their player and communicate silent messages that, at the end of the day, all more or less mean
the same thing: "Someone cares about how you're doing."

This year I'm not getting such messages, furtively or
otherwise. Still, I catch myself scanning the faces in the
crowd when I'm not involved in a hand. Were I playing
my best, I would use these frequent longeurs to study
the faces and hands and shoulders of my opponents, not
the faces and hands and breasts of attractive women on
the rail. Funny, isn't it, how attractive women and large
sums of cash often seem to collide at the same spot? This
is not to suggest that a nice lady I notice, a nearly six-
foot-tall Eurasian woman sporting black hot pants and a
tank-top the size of a cocktail napkin covering her won-
ders-of-modern-medicine décolletage, is an expensive
prostitute. But, it must be noted, she seems inordinately
fascinated with a diminutive fellow two tables to my left
who, every time he means to tip the attending waitress
exactly $1, takes great pains to extract from the pocket of
his nylon track pants a wad of hundred-dollar-bills the
size of your fist.

These kind of oblique mating rituals occur at the
World Series of Poker as naturally and openly as a male
peacock fans his tail feathers. But in addition to their os-
tensible aphrodisiacal quality, crisp hundreds, when
flashed properly, also serve notice to anyone who cares
to look that the possessor of such ready cash really truly
honestly doesn't care about the money he stands to win
or lose in this sweet little $5 million poker game. He's
got way too much of the smelly old stuff to be bothered.
This non-verbal message, of course, is a patent lie, the
same as betting into a pot with nothing but a busted
straight draw. Yet I see such "declarations" made at the
World Series of Poker regularly—almost as regularly as,
well, big bets being made by players holding nothing but

a busted straight draw. It's all part of the bluffing that's essential to getting paid.

As I idly search the eyes in the crowd, wondering which pair belong to someone immune to the allure of power and which belong to someone who has journeyed here to Las Vegas specifically in search of it, I notice, almost subconsciously, that I'm being stared at. From the periphery, to my right, on a sight-line between Taxi Ned and Carlos, I feel the unmistakable heat of an unwavering gaze locked on me.

I turn to look. It's my art-critic-cum-porno-fantasy dream girl reincarnated. It's J.

My eyes widen and my mouth opens in a most unpokerly way. It's J!

She's tracked me down here at Binion's Horseshoe because—because why? Because she had an epiphany last night, a stunning and inspiring moment of clarity in which she knew, she just *knew*, I am a man she couldn't let slip out of her life? Because she couldn't continue living without at least one more of my kisses? Because she finally understood that love is stronger than her secret compulsions?

In the millisecond it takes me to consider the myriad explanations for J's stunning arrival at the World Series of Poker, I notice that her gorgeous face is indeed fixed upon mine—but that her eyes are looking through me, on another man, who sits at the table behind me with his back nearly touching mine.

And then I notice that this ravishing brunette staring beyond me is not J at all.

After I stop shuddering, I make a mental note: Get your contact lenses and your psyche checked upon returning to Los Angeles.

For the first 90 minutes of level three, I don't hold any hands worth playing. Between furtive glances at the J impostor at the rail and larcenous raids on unprotected blinds, I fold innumerable trouble hands, like A-4, K-9, and even K-Q in early position. Unless the flop hits starting cards like these perfectly, you usually end up possessing the second best hand, which, in a poker game, tends to be about as useful as picking place horses to win. It takes discipline worthy of a dominatrix with a military school upbringing to watch everyone around you getting involved, winning and losing—*playing*—while you pass, pass, pass, observing the human folly from an ascetic distance. But in a true and just world—as opposed to the one we currently inhabit—such virtue, the good books tell us, is sure to be rewarded. The meek shall inherit the chips, and the unworthy will be relegated to the gloomiest corners of purgatory, where someone always beats your top pair with a slightly better kicker.

And thus, the poker gods decreed, it shall be so. Right?

Right! Either my patience is finally being rewarded or I'm unwittingly fulfilling that great cliché about lucky-in-love-unlucky-in-cards that my father likes to use to explain his reticence to take a risk on anything involving the vagaries of chance. T is gone with my money, N has a boyfriend, and J has dispatched a remarkably lifelike cyborg replicant of herself to torment me from a small distance. Yes, it's all true. But I finally have a hand!

The Invisible One in seat #9 opens the pot from first position for the minimum bet, $200. I look down at my cards and find J-J. At this point, to eyes weary of espying starting hands better suited to doubling down at blackjack than playing no-limit hold 'em, two jacks looks like a sequential royal flush. I raise $800. The Viper, having previously read me correctly as living the wastrel's life of crime, has come over the top of my last two raises.

This time he considers his hand for a few seconds before acting. Then he sneers slightly and says, "I raise." He matches my bet and raises another $1,600. Sensing impending drama, the rest of the table quickly folds. They're eager to have the gambling equivalent of rink-side seats at a hockey game when the home team, down by three goals, puts its "enforcer" on the ice for some poetic retribution against the other team's stylish Czech wing looking to pad his hat trick statistics. They can smell blood.

So can Mr. Invisible. He folds.

Now the action is back to me. It's that time again, ladies and gentleman! It's time to play everyone's favorite game, Fold or Raise.

Fold or raise. Raise or fold. What shall I do?

Well, if he's attempting a steal—and the Viper is a good enough player to pick the optimal spot to pull off such a pernicious maneuver—I should re-raise him. End of drama.

If he's not stealing—that is, if he's betting his hand for value, I should fold, since I am at best a tiny favorite against the A-K he might have in this situation, and at worst a big underdog against the bigger pocket pair he could well have in this situation.

Of course, there's the small chance he's feeling a bit too frisky with something like a pair of nines, in which case *I'm* a big favorite.

So, which is it, I wonder.

This is one of those moments that occur regularly in poker games, one of those moments when you wish you possessed x-ray vision or, at the very least, a Nostradamus-like ability to foresee the future. The great players seem to have mortgaged their souls—or at least a sizable part of their personalities—to be blessed with such gifts. They may be one-dimensional, emotionally barren, obsessive-compulsive weirdos. But at a card table they can see forever.

Regrettably, I possess none of this magic. I'm forced to rely on far less spectacular talents.

I carefully assess the Viper, who appears to me inscrutable as ever, a confident young Asian man with a slight air of menace and danger about him, as though he were a recently initiated member of some terribly violent gang of automatic-weapon-toting thugs intent on cornering the Los Angeles heroin trade. (Hell, for all I know he's on full scholarship to UCLA, where he's completing his residency in anesthesiology.) What's there in seat #2, besides a *tabula rasa*?

Look carefully, beneath the obvious and the apparent, I urge myself. Find the answer.

Has the cumulative ennui of folding for 90 minutes clouded my judgment? Or is it something I sense in his breathing that convinces me he's trying to take advantage of me? Or have I come to a dark bleak point in my life where I secretly believe *everyone* is trying to take advantage of me?

At the moment I don't know conclusively, which is the problem with this vexing game called poker. One too seldom *knows*. If you require further evidence that poker in many ways operates as a neat little metaphor for life, I submit the foregoing. We all wish at one time or another to answer the essential questions Paul Gauguin proposed to explore in paint more than 100 years ago, while he was in Tahiti, sating his appetite for underaged Polynesian nymphs: Who am I and, tell me, where am I going? Based on the success of "psychics" and tarot-card interpreters and other charlatans of the seeing-into-the-future industry, more than a few people yearn to be told, to have some certainty, that the path they are traveling will lead to Valhalla or, at the very worst, a nice home in the suburbs and a membership at the country club.

I'm generally not interested in such prognostications.

I don't want someone to tell me what lies ahead. Discovering the bumps and pits, the summits and vistas, on my own is perhaps the greatest thrill in being alive. If your life's story were indeed preordained by some master author with a taste for black humor, would you really want to know how it turns out? I wouldn't. I want to unravel the mystery slowly and never find out how it ends.

That said, when playing in the World Championship of poker, particularly after you've had your pair of jacks re-raised by a tricky Vietnamese dude, it would occasionally be nice to get a sneak preview.

Alas, with none forthcoming, I decide the Viper is stealing. Now, I use the word "decide" here loosely, in the way one might "decide" between a night of unspeakable debauchery with Juliette Binoche instead of Nicole Kidman. As with so many poker questions, the correct answer is not always patently clear, and the brave player must allow art to take up where science leaves off. Of course, true artists are rarer than an Orthodox Jew hog farmer. The great ones, the men who win multiple World Championships and dazzle onlookers with their otherworldly vision, are gambling's version of Bach and Michelangelo and Wordsworth. The rest of us must be content with making feeble lunges at the sublime, saddled with the knowledge that we cannot capture whatever it is that separates the genius from the anonymous herd of earnest toilers. Just as one must eventually make peace with the realization that truly knowing what occurs in the mind of another—like, one's lover of three years—is epistemologically impossible, a very good but not great poker player must make peace with the fact that he can't truly be certain of anything. And that playing in such a state of doubt is fine.

I have not yet reached that state of blissful equanimity. I want to feel like Kasparov when he stands over a chessboard, Woods when he strides to the 18th tee, Chan when he gets heads-up with a 2-1 chip lead. I want guarantees.

Maybe I'm playing the wrong game. Or maybe—and this is far more likely—I haven't yet fully digested the Facts of Life, cheerless as they may be.

The Heisenberg Uncertainty Principle aside, I convince myself that the Viper is attempting a courageous steal with his bold re-raise. "I raise," I say flatly, sliding $4,000 more into the pot.

Possibly faster than it takes for a synapse to traverse the distance of one microscopic cell, the Viper moves in his entire stack.

Whoops.

I think for about five seconds before folding. My brief reverie has nothing to do with "should I or shouldn't I?"—clearly I'm going to fold. Instead, I take a moment to reflect on What Can Be Learned From This Mistake. The answer is: I don't rightly know at the moment, other than, perhaps, I have a highly developed talent for talking myself into seeing things that aren't really there. It's a wonder, a miracle actually, that I've yet to be converted to some obscure cult whose primary article of faith is the periodic appearance of the Virgin Mary in the burned-out lightbulbs on the Stardust Casino's marquee (right below the advertisement for the $9.95 steak and lobster special). Silly me. I should have been a character in Aesop's Fables, The Blundering Poker Dog, a confused bloodhound who constantly picks up the wrong scent and follows it directly to the secret lair of hungry carnivores much larger and meaner than he. Moral of this story? Don't re-raise a ferocious Vietnamese dude when he comes over the top of two previous early-position raisers.

As I disconsolately toss my now worthless jacks into the muck, I mutter (just loudly enough for the Viper to hear) about how lucky this guy is to hold a big hand whenever I get kings. This is a lie, of course, the kind of "innocent" malfeasance that occurs regularly at a poker table—particularly when someone pulling in a pot declares he had been the proud owner of two specific cards, yet for some reason that's never made clear he wasn't proud enough to actually support his claim with a public viewing of his face-down masterpiece. (This common stunt is typically accompanied by the words "Now, you fellas know I wouldn't lie at the poker table," followed by much forced laughter and a variety of unwitty ripostes that would have Sheridan spinning in his scandalous grave.)

Being a good and prolific liar is not only acceptable at the poker table, it's celebrated. One could argue that this fact alone makes poker tournaments an intrinsically bad place, where the forces of evil have overrun the guardposts of morality. Morality, though, is often just thinly veiled envy. The alternative argument goes something like this: The fact that lying is rewarded makes poker tournaments an intrinsically good place, where the hypocrisies of the world at large have no currency. Say what you will about Bill Clinton's choice of phallus-slurping interns, his refined ability to lie blithely and convincingly under immense pressure was both dazzling and enlightening. And in some quarters quietly applauded.

Poker players whose bald mendacity garners admiration and respect from the targets of their untruthfulness remind me of certain corrupt Louisiana politicians whose satisfied constituents faithfully return them to office for consecutive terms of institutional thievery, even after the rascals have been indicted for numerous breaches of the law, not to mention common sense. It's all part of the game, goes the thinking. The advantage in poker is that there's never the threat of some do-gooding special prosecutor to ruin the party. If you lie often and well enough at a poker tournament, you won't end up sharing a prison cell with a large man named Bubba who has an unseemly interest in the way your posterior fits into your Department of Corrections workpants. No, you'll eventually be handed a pile of cash and an engraved gold bracelet from Neiman-Marcus.

I'm hoping the Viper will rise to the bait and reveal what in fact he had. It won't lessen the sting of losing more than $6,000 on the hand, but at least I can kid myself into thinking I've purchased a morsel of information, albeit at a price that makes black truffles seem as economical as lima beans.

"Yes, I'm lucky," the Viper replies, with just a bit too much vitriol for my sensitive ears. "Very lucky man." He flips over the two black aces that have brought him the mound of chips he's now stacking into perfect pillars of accomplishment. "Always lucky."

The subtext of his proclamation, for those not well-versed in the peculiarities of English as a Second Language Filtered Through the Mind of a Poker Player, is this: *You can call me lucky all you want, but it's skill—skill, you ignorant fool—that wins me chips, not random good fortune.*

He's right, and I don't disagree with him. I've often heard aggrieved losers sincerely accuse winners of being "so fucking lucky," as if extracting such a confession from the victor will somehow dull the pain of losing. All this noise is simply code for, "I played better than you did and so by all rights I should have won," which suggests a naïve belief that poker, or any other realm of this universe, is a smoothly efficient meritocracy. I have a two-word refutation for anyone still harboring this juvenile illusion: Kenny G.

But accusing the Viper of being the fortunate recipient of dumb luck is not what our exchange was really about. At least not to me. He got what he wanted out of our brief colloquy: a chance to defend his unassailable honor. And I got what I wanted: a "free" peek at his cards.

It all goes under the heading of Bluffing Your Way to the Truth.

I continue to mutter, sounding vaguely like Yosemite Sam without the accent, but it's only because I'm mad at myself, not the whims of fate or whomever or whatever decides which cards an expectant poker player will get to work with. I could have saved $5,600 by immediately folding when the Viper sent me the message (entirely clear in retrospect!) that he had the goods. Now I'm back down to $8,500 and officially steamed.

Poker chips are like a reputation: difficult to earn and easy to lose. When you've spent six hours diligently building up your homestead one crusty brick at a time, only to see it crumble to its foundations in one hot gust of ill fortune or bad judgment, the result can be as demoralizing as having your nearly completed Great American Novel lost to a power surge. If the World Series of Poker is the Olympic marathon of card games—and no other tournament requires four days of heroic effort—then an early catastrophic loss feels like the 26-mile race has been cruelly amended to 31 miles of brutal moraines.

It's one thing to give a weak player a few extra chips to play with; it's entirely another to subsidize world-class mendicants. Though legendary stories of some determined soul coming back from the dead, grinding his single remaining chip into a championship title, inspire tournament competitors never to give up, the odds against are overwhelming. After losing all my winnings-and-then-some to the Viper, more than my bankroll feels crushed.

My spirit aches, too.

But I don't quit—not yet. My stubbornness, I suppose, could be attributed to the never-give-up ethos instilled in all young boys weaned on *Rocky* movies and Joe Montana two-minute drills. Even poker players who know they're going to lose tend to pugnaciously adopt the Jake La Motta response to getting his face pulverized by Sugar Ray Robinson, immortalized in *Raging Bull*: "You didn't knock me down, Ray. You didn't knock me down."

That's how I feel at the moment: bloodied, bruised, damaged, but still standing.

Plus, the J impostor seems to have been joined by a cute friend I catch staring at me every time I look her way. (Of course, it could be my contact lenses again.) That great inspirer of folly and achievement, the male ego, won't allow me to go gently into that neon night.

Rather than allowing a destructive moment of self-hatred to wash over me like so much battery acid, I channel the steam I envision seeping out of my ears into pleasant standard-issue aggression. Since the poker table is one of the rare places in our "civilized" society where precisely directed rage often produces benefits, not lengthy prison sentences, my angst manifests in a short but profitable blind-raiding mission, and I churn my stake back to $9,500 as the session ends.

During the one-hour dinner break, while the majority of the remaining field (about 350 players) descends on the Horseshoe buffet to gorge on fried pork chops and trade unimaginably dull stories about how unlucky they got (or variations on this general theme), I retreat to my room and attempt to visualize how I'm going to double through two or three times and get back in contention. The problem is I can't see it.

The only images in my mind's eye are of loss. Lost love. Lost dreams. Lost poker chips.

You don't need a sports psychologist or a late-night-television motivational coach hawking overpriced self-realization videotapes to know this is a sure way to self-realize yourself into failure. Images of my pocket queens holding up all-in against Ned's A-10 should be dancing in my head; instead, I envision T doing unmentionable things with her new boyfriend.

I take the bouquet of herbs I brought for N and throw them in the trash.

Something wonderful must happen during Level Four if I'm to remain in the 2000 World Series of Poker. Well, that's not entirely true. I could pay my blinds and antes (at this level, there's a $25 toll every hand to accompany the $100 and $200 blinds), never get involved in a hand, and die a prolonged emphysematic death, wheezing and gasping down to the felt. But one of the first lessons a successful tournament competitor learns is that there's practically no difference between finishing in 53rd or 453rd place; one looks more impressive than the other, but neither pays any money. The idea in gambling tournaments, be they conducted with dice, dominos, or 52 cards, is to quickly amass hordes of ammunition or quickly go down trying. Some players claim they'd rather be the first eliminated from a tournament than finish one out of the money; it feels less painful, less like "so close yet so very far," and the many hours wasted earning nothing could be better used beating up on weak live games or making a return visit to the buffet.

Now, a seasoned tournament player keenly avoids senseless kamikaze missions, particularly those bombing runs whose misguided purpose is to capture the chip lead from the moment the tournament begins. It's a long war, after all. But to purposefully dodge conflict merely to "survive" a few hours before you perish is antithetical to the point of playing a poker tournament. You want to be the last man standing. Or in the case of the 2000 Main

Event, one of the last 45. And the only way to do that is to win a few fights.

When you're relatively short-stacked, as I am at this point, you should, in fact, be actively seeking conflicts. This does not mean brashly provoking the unwanted ire of the table bully, goading him into a position where he has no choice but to smack you upside your impudent head. The "trick," if you can call something so obvious by that name, is to get your chips—*all* your chips—involved in a gruesome conflict in which you have some sort of demonstrable advantage, no matter how small.

Experienced players might read the preceding passage and wonder, "Isn't that what you're *always* trying to do in no-limit poker?"

I don't think so. Watch the great champions early in the Main Event. They assiduously avoid letting a lesser player have a shot at all their chips, even if they, the champions, have a small short-term edge. The great ones seem to figure (correctly, in my estimation) that their long-term edge is even greater. From what I've seen, early in a long poker tournament like the World Series of Poker, superior players prefer to win a bunch of small decisions rather than engaging in a coin flip for all the money. Mathematical types call this "reducing volatility." Good ol' boys who grew up playing in the back rooms of West Texas saloons refer to this concept as "not giving a sucker a break."

When you're up against someone who plays better than you, particularly after the flop, you're usually better off forcing an all-in confrontation before the community cards hit the table—even if you suspect you're at best 50-50 to have the stronger hand. Chris Ferguson, who, despite the machinations of myself and 510 other earnest contestants, will go on to win the 2000 World Series of Poker (and the $1.5 million first prize), employs this tactic against the runner-up, T. J. Cloutier, during the largest poker pot in tournament history. Realizing Cloutier, the all-time leading money winner at the World Series, is the superior player, Ferguson calls his opponent's all-in raise holding only A-9. Having played in numerous tournaments with Mr. Ferguson, who is popularly known as "Jesus" because of his long tresses and facial hair, I can tell you he knows he doesn't have the best hand. When T. J. Cloutier re-raises all-in (with two players left holding an almost equal amount of chips), Chris Ferguson fears he might be drawing dead to three cards. (In fact, he is; Cloutier has A-Q.) But he knows he might plausibly have stumbled into a 50-50 proposition— two "over cards" versus a smaller pair. Reducing the World Championship of Poker to what amounts to heads versus tails may seem wanly unpoetic. But Ferguson accurately assesses the circumstances and discovers, ironically, that the optimal way for him to win at this point in the tournament is to gamble.

I once happened upon Amarillo Slim and nine other hopeful punters playing showdown poker for $1,000 a hand. The winner of this game, in which the only skill is counting out ten $100 bills from your bankroll, instantly had a large enough stake to buy into the Main Event. "What are you doing?" I inquired, amused that so many ostensibly sophisticated poker players would reduce their World Series dreams to this.

"It's called gambling," Slim replied. "You ought to try it sometime."

I remember Slim's advice when, on the ultimate hand at the 2000 World Series of poker, a nine falls on the river. Chris Ferguson's underdog A-9 suddenly seems like an excellent hand. What appears upon first consideration to be a lousy call is, upon further investigation, a particularly wise call—especially from one who is able to see beyond an isolated battle and understand the larger campaign.

With this ethos in mind, I'm looking for a spot to slide in my whole stack—sticking it in, according to the evocative parlance—in hopes of having it slide back to me with a like amount of chips piled beside it. And preferably the sooner the better. Doubling through when you've got $9,000 is a lot more meaningful than when you've got, say, $3,000.

My problem is I have neither the cards nor the position to make a stand. Either the Viper or Carlos (and, of course, Ned) seem to be involved in most of the hands before the action comes around to me. Like one who is forced to endure "Falcon Crest" reruns when he'd rather be reading Jim McManus in *Harper's* describing his once-in-the-history-of-Western-civilization march to the World Series of Poker final table, I'm an unwilling voyeur. I mean, I like to watch as much as the next guy. But what I really want to do at the moment is dive in and get messy.

What I see next is both horrifying and magnificent, Gericault's *Raft of the Medusa* realized in cards and chips. I can hardly believe what I'm seeing, so ineffably beautiful is the image. But I am dismayed, too. Because once again I'm witnessing a poker hand that proves beyond a scintilla of a doubt that I will not, cannot, should not, win the 2000 World Series of Poker.

The Viper, in early position, raises $800 with a few of what used to be my dear departed chips. Ned (naturally) calls. Carlos, slumping slightly in his chair, calls. Everyone else folds.

The flop comes 9-7-3 of various suits.

The Viper taps the table twice and says, "Check."

Ned looks at his cards to make sure they haven't changed in the past 15 seconds and says wearily, "I check."

Carlos frowns slightly, nods, and shuffles a stack of hundred-dollar chips in his café con leche fingers. He puts them down and switches to black-and-yellow $500 discs.

"Bet," he says, stacking $3,000 in front of him.

Ned, out of turn, throws up his hands in frustration.

The Viper draws deeply on his cigarette and mimics his Latin opponent's chip-shuffling prowess. "Call," he says, pushing forward several minarets of money.

Ned folds and says something irrelevant. Carlos blinks languidly.

"Two players," the dealer says, laying down a jack. Though this card fills an open-ended straight, I figure it's highly unlikely (though not impossible) that one of these good players is holding something like a suited 8-10.

The Viper, first to act, checks. I look him over: nothing. I can't tell if he's got a pair of aces or rapidly dying dreams.

Carlos, staring across the table, hesitates for a few seconds. Then he says, "I bet," and flips a $5,000 chip toward the pot.

Interesting. If Carlos has the best hand he's clearly not worried about letting the Viper get a cheap draw, or else he would have bet at least the size of the pot. If he himself is drawing—which I strongly doubt—he's wasting money. And if he's got a monster—three-of-a-kind, for instance—he's milking it for all it's worth.

The Viper looks over at Carlos and considers his options. Though he appears to the rest of the table—and particularly Carlos—perfectly calm, from my seat adjacent to him, I can see his leg pumping furiously beneath the tabletop, the manic energy bleeding out of his sandal-clad foot into the ash-stained carpet.

"Call," he says.

No one says anything, but all of us are thinking, "Wow, this is important." I mean, not in a Human Genome Project kind of way. But everyone sits up a little straighter. Everyone starts to mentally reconstruct the action. Everyone begins theorizing about what each of these titans actually has hidden face-down on the table. And, as gamblers are wont to do, everyone silently "predicts" what will happen next.

Which is this: The dealer peels off another three, pairing the board. The flop now reads 9-7-3-J-3. The Viper chews his lower lip, lowers his left hand from where it has been scratching his ear, and taps the table with his forefinger. "Check," he says flatly.

Carlos tucks his chin to his chest and surveys the pot. If he were wearing bifocals, Carlos would be peering over them. "Bet," he says, stacking out $7,000.

The Viper looks at his opponent with what can only be described as malice, as though this mild-mannered Spaniard had somehow insulted the rice vermicelli and beef tendons the Viper's mom has prepared for dinner. He fondles his chips, looking from Carlos to the pot, the pot to Carlos. Neither object moves.

"I raise," the Viper says, allowing just a hint of music to color his usual monotone. He matches the original $7,000 with $7,000 more.

Now Carlos is the one who looks mildly perturbed. He rubs the back of his head, mutters softly to himself in Spanish, and shifts in his seat, as though the plush cushions supporting his ass have suddenly turned to slate. Subtly, almost imperceptibly, he begins to shake his head "no."

I look at the Viper. His leg has stopped pumping.

I look back at Carlos. He sighs. He shakes his head. And then he smiles. "Good hand," he says, showing the two sevens he is folding.

"Folding a set?" Ned asks, incredulous.

"No good," Carlos says.

"He play with me before," the Viper says, showing the table his two nines. "He know I don't raise with nothing. He know I only raise with the nuts."

I'm stunned.

Set over set. You rarely see three-of-a-kind versus another three-of-a-kind in Texas hold 'em, and when you do in the no-limit variety of this game, someone invariably loses all of his chips.

The Viper had the courage and vision to check and call, check and call, and check once more on the end, certain he would have the opportunity to raise.

Carlos had the courage and discipline to fold a huge hand that could have won him an enormous pot, certain he was beat.

I have previously had to confront the awful knowledge that I will never sing like José Carerras, compose poetry like John Donne, or look even remotely like Brad Pitt. These are all disappointing realizations. But none of these small remorses feels quite as depressing as knowing I cannot play poker well enough to do what Carlos and the Viper just did.

And they're not even World Champions.

I officially give up after the epic Carlos versus Viper hand. Oh, I'm still in my seat, and I still mechanically put chips into the pot and generally conduct myself like someone who has played in a poker tournament or two. But my heart and mind, and probably my soul, have long since left this iniquitous gambling den. I'm somewhere far away, somewhere in the past, when I had a sweet auburn-haired lover who taught me to be true, to always be blessedly true.

A cocktail waitress asks me if I'd like anything to drink. I stare at her cascading red locks and try not to smile or cry.

"Nothing," I hear myself say. "I'm done."

She grins professionally and opens her mouth as

though she's about to say something. I imagine those lips, her lips, the ones that were once mine, kissing me.

And then she's gone.

I look down at my cards. Three days before Jim McManus will steal my dream for himself, three days before Chris Ferguson will get paid $1.5 million, three days before these two unrelated cards will make history, I see an ace and a nine staring back at me.

I put in my last $4,400 and feel my shoulders twitch with an involuntary shudder of pleasure. Until next year, no one will be able to bluff me again.

Also by Michael Konik

The Man With the $100,000 Breasts
and Other Gambling Stories

ISBN 0-929712-72-2 • PRICE $24.95

A fearless gambler who got breast implants to win a $100,000 bet. A hard-core dice shooter who turned a borrowed stake of $10,000 into $17 million. A marketing genius who developed a "900" line for selecting winners of NFL football games—and had his four-year-old son make the picks. These are some of the characters that populate Michael Konik's *The Man With the $100,000 Breasts and Other Gambling Stories*, the original collection of the renowned gambling writer's best magazine pieces.

Konik ushers readers into the arena of risk and reward, introducing them to the subculture of high rollers, hustlers, professional card counters, horse handicappers, and poker champions.

Entertaining and stylish, *The Man with the $100,000 Breasts and Other Gambling Stories* is a literary look inside the world of gambling.

Nice Shot, Mr. Nicklaus
Stories About the Game of Golf

ISBN 0-929712-03-X • PRICE $23.95

Golf-writer and hacker extraordinaire Michael Konik roams the golfing universe in this outstanding collection of stories about the game and its grandeur. Konik's intimate profiles take you inside the minds and motives of some of the biggest names in golf—John Daly and Phil Mickelson, Raymond Floyd and Jim Colbert, Helen Alfredsson and Laura Davies, Dave Pelz and Vince Gill, among them.

Nice Shot, Mr. Nicklaus also guides readers around the planet in search of exotic golf adventures, from Scotland and Spain to the United Arab Emirates and El Salvador. Konik chronicles his own misadventures in some of the world's quirkiest tournaments, writes eloquently and movingly about demeanor on the links, and, of course, caddies for Jack Nicklaus in the memorable title story.

About Huntington Press

Huntington Press is a specialty publisher of Las Vegas- and gambling-related books and periodicals. To receive a copy of the Huntington Press catalog, call 1-800-244-2224 or write to the address below.

Huntington Press
3687 South Procyon Avenue
Las Vegas, Nevada 89103